CONNECT

The Secret
To Generate Leads, Build Relationships,
And Dramatically Increase Your Sales

JOSH TURNER

LIONCREST
PUBLISHING

Contents

INTRODUCTION

The Power of Relationships

We spend our days in management—our time, our money, our employees, and even ourselves. But how often do we remember to manage our relationships?

Relationships, like stocks or bonds, are valuable assets. When mismanaged, or simply left to their own devices, they fall apart the moment we need to lean on them. But when relationships are carefully managed, they bring growth and prosperity.

Here's a famous example. In 2011, AOL acquired *The Huffington Post* for $315 million—less than six years after its launch. In a crowded field of agile competitors and award-winning journalists, how did *The Huffington Post* rise to the top? In a word, relationships—specifically, the relationships and connections cultivated by co-founder Arianna Huffington. In a 2011 article titled "Arianna Huffington: The Connector," *Vogue* magazine attributed Huffington's success to her uncanny ability to build relationships.

In any business, developing a powerful system for forming, nurturing, and sustaining relationships with prospects, business partners, and clients is essential.

But as our world changes, the nature of business relationships is changing too. Learning to harness new practices will allow you to build, refine and scale your business quickly. Relying on relationship-building techniques developed even five or ten years ago (let alone twenty or thirty or fifty) to connect with new customers will get you only one thing: left behind.

REDEFINING RELATIONSHIPS

The digital economy has changed the way we communicate, especially with potential customers. Sophisticated digital platforms and social marketing have made it easier than ever to identify potential customers, contact them, earn their trust, build a relationship, establish yourself as a leader in your space, and ask for a face-to-face sales meeting. But because we don't understand how to leverage these platforms and tactics for success, many of us still struggle to find new revenue, increase sales and grow our businesses.

Who can blame us? Learning new and unfamiliar practices can be intimidating. Doing what's always worked before is comforting—we already know how to do it, authorities have approved it, and even when it doesn't work, we can reassure ourselves that we've tried our best and "the market is just against us."

Unfortunately, what worked reasonably well just five years ago is woefully outdated and inadequate today. Sticking with old-school techniques means leaving sales (and money) on the table. It also means your competition eating your lunch when they figure out the new techniques before you, and establishing themselves as trusted industry leaders while you're still making cold calls.

Let's look at the difference between sticking with old-fashioned practices and learning current ones with a pair of business stories.

GENERATING NEW BUSINESS...THE OLD WAY

After years of working for a big payroll company, Sue Thompson left her position and started her own payroll service a few months ago. Ever since, she's been hustling every day to find new clients. She's doing all the stuff every sales guru says you should do: networking meetings, coffees and lunches, requests for introductions, chamber of commerce meetings, handing out business cards, even spending two days a week cold calling. But the results are coming way too slow.

After several months of sixty-hour workweeks, Sue has picked up a handful of clients. But now she's finding that as the demands of her paying clients grow, she has less time for prospecting and networking. And the few coffee meetings and sales lunches she still has time for don't seem to be yielding any new clients. Most of these meetings end with Sue and her new business connection agreeing to "keep in touch," but never actually connecting again.

By now, Sue is really tired. She thinks to herself, "There must be a better way." She realizes it's going to take a methodical commitment, and some sort of organized system or process, to stay in touch with these contacts and develop an ongoing business relationship with them. But she only has so much time for coffee and lunch meetings, which already take too much time and just aren't scalable.

Thinking about the future of her business, both short and long term, Sue begins to realize that servicing an existing client list and also making time to prospect for new business is impossible for her small company. Sadly, she considers folding her new venture and going back to work for a big payroll company.

Sue's story is all too common. She grew up in an era where sales managers preached old-school techniques. But the world is changing, and while Sue knows on some level she needs to change with it, she's just not sure how.

GENERATING NEW BUSINESS...IN THE DIGITAL ERA

Now let's look at a very different approach. Examine the story below and consider how a novel strategy makes all the difference.

Bob Sanders had a long career working for small and medium-sized construction companies. He knew that his skills were in demand, and that there was no shortage of companies that needed help. So he decided to set up his own construction consulting firm.

Prior to striking out on his own, Bob spent several years following the growing importance of digital media and social marketing. He knew that the right way to grow his business was not by attending networking events, going to chamber breakfasts, meeting potential clients for coffee, and handing out business cards to everybody he meets. Bob knew he could spend that same time much more effectively.

*So Bob set up his new firm's sales practices to leverage the new paradigm for generating sales leads and building a scalable business. Bob knew that it was absolutely possible to design a system to **bridge online with offline activities**, so that he could systematically build relationships with thousands of potential clients in a short amount of time. Bob was certain that he could take the old-school principles of networking and referrals, combine them with all of these new online tools and platforms, and create a powerful formula for generating leads consistently.*

Within just a few months, Bob had built an online networking and lead generation machine that was reaching an audience of targeted prospects fifteen times larger than his more old-fashioned competitors could reach. On top of that, the system allowed him to establish himself as a trusted resource and keep his name in front of these prospects on a regular basis, in a personal one-to-one manner. Bob now has a steady stream of new clients approaching him to discuss business and an outbound marketing effort that produces new opportunities every day. Now his biggest problem is hiring enough employees to handle all the business.

What these two parables illustrate is that face-to-face, in-person networking and relationship building takes a tremendous amount of time and effort. Every minute you spend driving to a coffee meeting and making small talk is time away from running and managing your business. And if that meeting doesn't result in a new paying client, it's essentially wasted time. The process is inefficient. You have to spend an inordinate amount of time and energy to reach a small number of potential clients.

Not only that, prospecting the old-fashioned way, in person or via cold calling, simply doesn't scale. It's impossible to go for coffee with a thousand prospects in a year. Heck, it's nearly impossible to go for coffee with a couple hundred, unless that's your only responsibility.

But when you leverage the power of the Internet, you find possibilities today that never existed before. Smart companies are using large, existing digital platforms to get their message out to thousands of potential customers all at the same time. Try doing that at Starbucks.

The only hurdle is that these technologies are new. Implementing those means learning specialized techniques you've never used before. But this is actually an advantage, because by reading this book and putting the plan into action, you will be getting a big jump on your competitors. By the time they figure out what you're doing, it will be too late for them to catch up.

WHAT THIS BOOK WILL TEACH YOU

This book will show you how to systematically develop relationships with thousands of cold prospects, converting them into warm leads over time, all done utilizing online tools you already have at your disposal. I'll teach you how to do this in a way that's easily scalable, primarily using LinkedIn and webinars.

You'll have more leads, better leads, more referrals, and you won't churn through prospects as fast. You'll be able to proactively pluck out the very best prospects and market to them in a specific way that culminates in a request for a phone call or a meeting, so that all you'll need to do is bring them into your sales process and close the sale. And once this system is in place and functioning, your marketing machine will be continually running in the background, so you'll finally be able to step off that roller coaster of constantly chasing the next sale.

This is not a book about social media. It is not a marketing textbook. It's a laser-focused recipe for finding new customers and winning their business in the digital age.

WHO WILL BENEFIT FROM THIS SYSTEM?

This book is for business owners, marketers and salespeople

in B2B companies. If you sell to other businesses, especially high-ticket products and services, then this book is for you. It doesn't matter what industry you're in; the tactics in this book are universal. For example, consulting services, enterprise software, design and construction, manufacturing, information products, law firms, CPAs, IT services, and many other industries have expensive products that require trust and a relationship to sell. Customers don't need a relationship with you to buy a $5 product, or to hire a graphic artist for $300 to design a one-off brochure, but they sure do need to know you if they're going to hire you to run their million-dollar monthly payroll.

Another important requirement is that your target customers must be companies or people that you can identify on LinkedIn. Although more and more businesses of all types are building an online presence, some industries simply aren't there yet. But if you can find them online, especially on LinkedIn, then this system will work for you.

YOU CAN DO THIS

If you're like most business people these days, you have more than a little trepidation about boldly entering the digital/social marketplace. Terms like "social media," "hashtags" and "analytics" may make you start sweating. But don't panic. By the time you're finished with this book you'll be ready to run a lead generation system that will amaze even the most tech-savvy online marketers. You'll understand it. You'll know how to use it. And soon you'll be on your way to generating hundreds of new leads to help take your business to a whole new level.

Let's get started.

CAVEMAN PSYCHOLOGY

Why do you almost always reject a sales call from a complete stranger? Why does cold calling yield such low results? What makes a prospect trust or mistrust you? And what's the best way to make sure they choose to trust you? The answers to these questions lie in millions of years of human evolution.

EVOLUTIONARY PSYCHOLOGY

There is a well-established branch of the social and natural sciences called evolutionary psychology. According to evolutionary psychologists, the brains of modern humans operate essentially the same way today as they did in the days of the caveman.

The brain evolves, but it evolves slowly. So while the modern human brain is very different than the brain of a Homo erectus on the African savanna one million years ago, it likely isn't so different from the brain of the early Homo sapiens. Although our brains were similar, our lives couldn't be more different. Early Homo sapiens spent their days running around with spears hunting mammoths, hiding from saber-toothed tigers, and clashing with other hostile clans. Survival in that prehistoric world depended in large part on how well individuals learned to evade danger, find food and shelter, work together and avoid hostile tribes. As our ancestors faced social and survival problems, they developed ways to adapt. Evolutionary psychology shows that these thousands of years of learned behavior eventually became ingrained as instinct—what we commonly refer to as "human nature."

Today, we don't need to sit down and puzzle out how to respond to many situations. Our instincts respond for us. And that doesn't just happen in fight-or-flight instances of fear or anxiety. Here's an example of how it shows up in a regular business scenario.

According to Harvard Ph.D. and behavioral scientist Dr. Samuel Bowles, as a consequence of tribal warfare, humans evolved to be more cooperative with members of their own tribe, and more hostile to members of unknown tribes.

So when a copier salesperson cold calls a purchasing manager whom he has never met, is it any surprise that the purchasing manager won't return the call? The salesperson is not in the purchasing manager's tribe—they don't work together, they don't know each other, so human nature warns the purchasing manager to be suspicious and not respond. Trying to set up a sales meeting with a cold prospect you've never met is difficult because you are literally trying to bypass thousands of years of ingrained human behavior.

So what's the solution?

Instead of working against human nature, learn to work *with* it. You'll see how the most effective way to turn cold prospects into warm leads is to gradually entice them to *join your clan.*

We'll talk more about *how* to do all this in a moment. First, let's look at *why* these switches work so well.

THE POWER OF FAMILIARITY

Humans are naturally wary of strangers. If a person we have never seen before approaches us on the street, we instantly put our guard up. However, if someone approaches who we've seen many times walking her dog around the neighborhood, our natural instinct will be to greet her with a smile, even if we've never met. Social psychologist Dr. Elliot Aronson writes in *The Social Animal*, "All other things being equal, the more familiar an item is, the more attractive it is. People prefer faces they've seen ten times to equally attractive faces they've seen only five times."

In other words, the more often people see something, the more comfortable they are with it *simply because they've seen it before.*

Why is this? Largely because of what's known as priming.

Priming works like this: When someone is exposed to a message repeatedly, they naturally start to believe and trust it. The higher the exposure, the deeper the trust.

The multi-billion dollar advertising industry is based on this very principle of priming. Aronson writes, "In the case of many consumer products, the public tends to buy a specific brand for no other reason than the fact that it is heavily advertised."

WORDS MATTER

Priming is not complicated. Many studies have shown that simply being primed with certain types of words can lead to a distinct change in behavior. A recent study published in the *Journal of Personality and Social Psychology* showed how priming with different types of words elicits different behaviors.

In this study, one group of students was primed with negative words, including: *rude, bother, disturb, intrude, annoyingly, interrupt, audaciously, brazen, impolitely, infringe, obnoxious, aggravating,* and *bluntly*. A second group of students was primed with positive words: *respect, honor, considerate, appreciate, patiently, cordially, polite, courteous, graciously, sensitively, behaved,* and *unobtrusively*. Then, still part of the experiment, each student was asked to go out into the hallway and fetch the professor, who was engaged in an important conversation with another colleague. The students primed with negative words were far more likely to rudely interrupt the professor's conversation.

This study and others like it show how vital it is to consider the *types* of words you use—especially with potential customers. Whether you're considering ad copy or personal messages to prospects, you want to use positive words. Words like *success, win, celebrate, affordable, profit, future, happy, prosperity, affluence,* and *wealth* will serve you and your clients much better than words like *fail, lose, disappear, shrink, competition, expensive,* and *losses.*

When you use these words is also important. Upbeat words and optimistic communications trigger positive emotions in the brain, which will cause your prospects to associate you with feeling good.

So to get that association going as soon as possible, start using positive words from the get-go. Open the relationship by communicating something positive or even inspirational. It can be as simple as, "Hey, thanks for connecting here. I'm impressed by what your company has accomplished."

Now what about the idea that the strongest marketing strategies play on the desire to avoid losing something? Oftentimes the promise of helping your client *not* lose what they already have can be more effective than the promise of future gains. But it is possible (and preferable) to couch this technique in positive language! If you constantly tell your potential clients that they are about to lose something, they'll start tuning you out, so make sure you stay positive even when talking about loss avoidance.

In addition to using positive language, make an effort to share positive content as well. Here's an example of how that works:

A client of ours owns a manufacturing company that sells equipment to the mining industry. There are a *lot* of negative topics and sad news in the mining industry—mining accidents, lawsuits, environmental controversies, protesters, negative publicity and news reports, and so on. If we were to focus on those negative headlines in the communications we write for this client, their readers and customers would get depressed about the shape of the mining industry. Worse, they'd associate the company giving them mining news—our client—with their own feelings of depression, and probably not support or buy from that company. Our client would be sunk!

So instead, when we write this client's communications we try to find a great success story, or talk about rising ore prices, or favorable legislation, or charitable donations to local communities. There is always good news, even if you have to look hard to find it, and focusing on that good news will help your potential customers associate you (the source of the good news) with the good feelings they get reading it.

SET YOURSELF UP AS A LEADER

It's not enough to simply "prime the pump." To really get the best results, your prospects need to view you as a leader in your space. Why is that? To break it down to the core, let's take a look at another Harvard University study. In this study, a lecturer presented a speech to two different groups of students about the importance of arithmetic. To one group, the presenter was introduced as an award-winning scholar from a prestigious research university. To the other group, the presenter was introduced as a dishwasher in a restaurant. As you might imagine, the students responded much more strongly to the "professor" than to the "dishwasher."

So if your prospects see you as the dishwasher, you're facing an uphill battle to convince them to do anything. You have to establish yourself as an expert or an authority in the field. Luckily, there are some relatively simple steps you can take to position yourself and your business as real leaders in your industry. We'll cover these steps in a later chapter.

EARN THEIR TRUST BY NOT SELLING THEM

Relationships are all about trust. If you want people to trust you, you have to keep them from thinking that you're just another salesperson trying to separate them from their money. So the best way to prime somebody for a sales conversation is not what most salespeople typically do; that is, telling them all about your company and your products.

So if you shouldn't talk about your company and your products, what should you talk about?

Easy: Talk about *them*. If you know their business well, give them information pertinent to that business. If you don't know their business well, ask them about it! People love talking about their businesses. Explore their needs and desires with them, and use your expertise to share ways to meet those needs. Sales will come later—right now your job is to earn their trust, and the way to do that is to give them everything you can without asking for anything back. Their instinct will be to look for the *quid pro quo* behind your words, so flip the script and don't have one for them to find.

Now that you have a beginning understanding of human nature and why it works the way it does, we're going to look at the specifics of how to achieve the objectives we discussed in this chapter. In the coming chapters we'll explain exactly how to use tools like LinkedIn groups and strategic messaging campaigns to turn cold prospects into warm leads, establish trust upfront, and place yourself as a leader in your industry. We'll also explore some examples, case studies, and success stories that demonstrate the power of this process. Let's dive in.

THE PROBLEMS WITH OLD-SCHOOL MARKETING

Just fifteen years ago, marketing and selling were much different than they are today. The Internet hadn't yet developed into its current state, and the ability to connect with a massive audience of targeted prospects was available only to major corporations with huge marketing budgets.

Today, marketing, selling, and the Internet could not be more closely intertwined. These days, even a solopreneur on a tight budget can leverage online tools to reach an audience of international clients.

But what even *is* marketing now? The game has changed so much that definitions from even a few years ago don't fit anymore. For instance, Wikipedia defines marketing as:

"The process of communicating the value of a product or service to customers, for the purpose of selling that product or service."

That definition is outdated. If you're a B2B company and your marketing is solely focused on communicating the value of your product or service, you are missing a key part of the equation. Marketing in the digital age requires a different strategy.

We now have widespread mainstream digital platforms that allow you to put your marketing message in front of exactly the right people. But here's the catch: If you use that technology simply to tell people about the value of your product or service, you'll get an extremely low response rate. People will tune you out. Even the right people are so saturated with that kind of marketing that they won't even look twice at yours. No, the true power of technology in marketing is relationship building.

Remember the objectives from the last chapter? Instead of just trying to sell products, if you use these tools to first build an online relationship, then establish trust and position yourself as a leader, you will almost never have a cold call in your life.

Still, the old-school marketer might argue, "Who has time to do all that networking with even a few hundred prospects, let alone several thousand?" And that's a valid question.

You remember Sue and her payroll service from the introduction of this book. Doing things the old-fashioned way, well, it just wasn't cutting it. Sue's been trying the relationship-building route by networking and meeting prospects over coffee. Her interactions with people feel genuine, but she can already see that the numbers just don't add up. There is a limit to how many coffee meetings she can schedule, and it's not very many. And most of her meetings don't result in new clients anyway. Her work doesn't scale. What Sue (and other old-school marketers) is missing is a systematic approach for combining both the social and psychological principles that turn prospects into customers *and* the new online tools that can reach tens of thousands of potential prospects.

Integrating these two seemingly-different approaches is known as Systematic Relationship Marketing. It is this process of using these new online tools, combined with classic social and psychological principles, which turns cold prospects into warm leads. It works like magic. So why are so few people doing it?

OLD HABITS DIE HARD

You'd be hard-pressed to find a legitimate company that's not doing something to promote their products or services online. The Internet is arguably the most powerful business tool since the invention of the telephone. But sadly, most companies aren't using it effectively, so they simply aren't getting the results they want or expect. Why is that?

In an article titled "The Power of the Internet," marketing guru and blogger Jason Thibeault wrote that the power of the Internet is that it enables the average person to have a voice that can be heard by thousands. In other words, the

Internet gives everybody a megaphone. And when you have a megaphone, you want to start shouting things through it.

Most business people will consider two options for their Internet Megaphone Shouting Campaign:

1. The kind of marketing and advertising they've been exposed to all their life. "It's worked so far, right? Why fix what isn't broken?"

2. The kind of marketing and advertising they're currently seeing on the Internet. "Everyone else is doing it, so we should too!"

More times than not, the marketing and advertising we are accustomed to, online and offline, is *interruption marketing*. Interruption marketing is exactly what it sounds like: marketing designed to interrupt whatever you're doing, grab your attention and direct it toward a product. This includes banner ads, pop-ups, radio commercials, Google ads, magazine ads, billboards, telemarketers, trade show booths, Facebook posts, television commercials, and on and on.

Our brains associate these types of communications with advertising and marketing—we know *instantly* they are trying to sell us something. We're very accustomed to the constant bombardment of commercials, billboards, and Internet ads. So when we think about how to promote our businesses, our brains automatically jump to interruption marketing because we've seen so much of it already. Remember from last chapter:

our belief and trust in something is hugely influenced by how often we've already seen it.

Unfortunately, interruption marketing is an old-school marketing tactic that frankly doesn't work very well anymore—if it ever really did. Imagine someone following you around with a megaphone and interrupting you with product pitches every two minutes. You'd tune them out (or smash the megaphone!) pretty darn quick. And that's exactly what potential customers do online—they tune out the ads or block them entirely.

But because your brain has seen these interrupting ads so many times, it assumes they *must* work. So you think, "If only I can come up with the right message and copy for my new ad, people will see how great we are and will be beating our door down to hire us." And when that fails, you think that Internet marketing just doesn't work for your business.

Internet marketing isn't the problem. The problem is that your *approach* is based on old beliefs and outdated ways of doing things. Buying ads for the sake of buying ads will not get you the results you want.

Instead, we all need to change our approach to how to interact with prospects. The next chapter will begin to show you how.

THREE

THE NEW MARKETING BLUEPRINT

Through modern digital platforms liked LinkedIn, any marketing professional or business owner can have their voice heard by literally thousands of people. The key to Internet marketing success is to know what to say, how often to say it, and where to say it.

The program described in this book will revolutionize your B2B marketing efforts by helping you develop more warm leads than you imagined possible. This system will walk you through the steps to do the following:

1. Identify prospects

2. Create a community to appeal to those prospects

3. Reach out to them in a strategic way

4. Bring them into your network

5. Develop a relationship with them

6. Establish yourself as a leader they can trust

7. Keep your name in front of them on an ongoing basis in a way that creates value and comfort for them

8. Gradually work them through a messaging process that culminates in a call to action (CTA)

By following the steps of this system, you will guarantee a much higher response rate to your CTAs than typical or old-school marketing tactics could get. We then combine this process with the superpower of webinars to turbo-charge your results.

Here's why this system works so well:

Instead of targeting just few dozen potential clients through face-to-face networking and in-person meetings, our system allows you to target and reach literally *thousands* of potential clients. It's almost infinitely scalable, and it works continuously to provide a constant stream of new prospects, so your sales pipeline won't dry up when you get busy.

HOW LINKEDSELLING WAS BORN

I started using LinkedIn in 2006, when I was the CFO of a construction and manufacturing firm in St. Louis. At that time,

LinkedIn was relatively new and only had about six million members; today it has hundreds of millions of members and is growing exponentially. When the recession hit the US economy in 2008, the company I was working for was hit pretty hard, and by 2009 was unfortunately forced to shut its doors.

I was out of a job, but I knew I had marketable skills. So I began using LinkedIn to market my services as a freelance CFO and finance pro. I was an early adopter of LinkedIn so I knew it pretty well, but I put myself through a crash course to learn even more. Soon I created a LinkedIn campaign for myself to market my skills as a freelancer.

Along the way I created my own LinkedIn group, currently called Small Biz Forum, which is still active today. (You can join the conversation by visiting **LinkedSelling.com/SmallBizForum**.) I invited CEOs and other top-level business owners and executives to join, and I provided value to them by regularly posting general business information and resources that I thought would be valuable to that audience. I rarely used Small Biz Forum as a sales tool for my own business. Instead, I posted general business content about human resources, small business insurance, employee morale, sales and marketing, productivity and time management, strategic planning, cost reduction and improving efficiency, and so on. I would never directly pitch my freelance CFO services, but I made it clear what kind of work I did.

As the LinkedIn group continued to grow, I began getting more freelance job offers than I could handle. I soon realized that by being the leader of the popular Small Biz Forum I was gaining a reputation around town as a credible, knowledgeable CFO and business leader. Furthermore, by regularly posting valuable content in the group I was keeping my name in front of thousands of powerful business execs who could hire me or refer me. So when the need for a finance executive came up at a St. Louis company, I was the one they thought of first. It was remarkable. And as this continued, I began to see the principles we discussed in the first chapter at work: by establishing myself as a leader, building trust through sharing value with no strings attached, and keeping my name in front of my audience without being pushy, I had created relationships that brought me more ecstatic clients than I knew what to do with.

As I started to realize the power of this system, I began working hard to refine it, improve it, and expand it. Then in 2011, I had a couple of clients who saw what the system was doing for my business and thought it might work for them as well. They asked my opinion and I gave them some thoughts on how they could go about creating their own LinkedIn campaigns. After listening, a couple of them said, "How about we just hire you to do that for us?" And that's when Linked-Selling was born and where things really took off. In 2012 we launched our online training program Linked University. Since then, between our agency LinkedSelling and training program Linked University, we've helped thousands of businesses skyrocket their sales using LinkedIn, and this book is designed to make *your* business one of the next ones to do the same.

IT'S NOT ONE OR THE OTHER, IT'S BOTH

One important note here: once you start using my system to harness the marketing potential of the Internet, you don't then have to abandon everything else. Face-to-face networking and in-person meetings still have tremendous value and will always play a part in your marketing strategy. You just won't have to rely *only* on those things anymore! Instead, with this system you'll limit your face-to-face meetings to bona fide warm leads with whom you've already established trust. So when it comes to online vs. offline marketing and prospecting, it's not a case of doing one or the other; you'll do both. You'll just do them better and scale them bigger.

BUT I'M NOT TECH SAVVY!

As noted above, technology has advanced and progressed *freaky* fast. Learning how to work with it can be like learning a whole new language. As a result, a lot of people, especially executives and businesspeople with decades of experience in traditional marketing, tend to feel intimidated by or skeptical of this new type of tech-central, Internet-heavy social marketing at first. You may be one of those people. The idea of taking so much of your marketing online might have you shaking in your shoes. You may not know where to start—or even if you want to.

That's okay. Really. I get that this can seem overwhelming, and so I designed this system to be simple and user-friendly. With a little time and focus, you can learn everything you need to feel completely comfortable with the system. You don't need any technical expertise, social media know-how, or above-average computer skills. All you need is the desire to do it and this book to show you how.

We'll start digging into the step-by-step process in the next chapter. But first, check out the case study below. The results you'll see in it are not a fluke. Many businesses easily achieve comparable sales results by learning my system, and yours can too!

· · · · · · · CASE STUDY · · · · · ·
U.S. Spray Foam

U.S. Spray Foam is a nationwide supplier of spray foam equipment. Their primary business is renting professional spray foam gear to contractors and homeowners, as well as providing training. Historically, most of their business has come through their website via Google traffic. Looking to grow and take a more proactive approach to developing new business, they asked the question, "Where can we find and reach our best prospects, and how can we go about targeting them to generate qualified leads?"

U.S. Spray Foam owner Corey McDonald worked with the LinkedSelling team to identify the following ideal prospect profiles: general contractors, commercial contractors, project managers, construction management firms, home builders, remodelers, and estimators. Using LinkedIn's Advanced People Search, we quickly identified over 107,000 ideal prospects in the United States. With that large of a prospect base, there was no doubt the campaign would generate a flow of qualified leads literally for years to come.

THE CAMPAIGN PLAN

Given the massive size of the construction market, a fairly direct approach made the most sense. Contractors are always happy to take a look at another bid, and sometimes urgently need additional options to consider. So getting in the door was going to be relatively easy for U.S. Spray Foam.

With that in mind, we structured a LinkedIn campaign to go after exactly the right prospects. The company wanted us to funnel leads to sales reps based on different market segments, so we structured the campaign around the sales reps' LinkedIn accounts. The system we devised with McDonald and his team began delivering weekly batches of targeted messages from each sales rep to the prospects in that rep's segments.

THE RESULTS

The campaign started generating leads in the first week, and it hasn't let up since.

On average it's generated 23.4 new leads per month. And these are qualified prospects with both short and long-term needs. Many of the leads have resulted in immediate sales opportunities. And nearly all of them have built the foundation for lasting relationships that will generate hundreds of thousands in revenue over their lifetime. McDonald also noted that "the long-term outlook from these leads is awesome... most of the projects these conversations lead to have been the biggest we've been involved in."

With my system in place, your business could have the same kind of tremendous results. In the next chapter, I'll show you how. You ready? Let's do this.

SETTING UP A LINKEDIN CAMPAIGN

Let's start this at the very beginning.

What is LinkedIn?

LinkedIn.com is an online business network where you can connect with other professionals: people that you've worked with, people that you're friends with through work, peers in your industry, people you know, or people you would like to know. If Facebook is for your personal network—friends and family—LinkedIn is for your business network.

LinkedIn is an enormous platform and it's getting bigger. At the time of this writing, LinkedIn membership is approaching half a billion people, and the company's stated goal is to reach three billion total members. According to internal company usage stats, 40% of members check LinkedIn daily.

The people who use LinkedIn are decision makers in their organizations. According to independent market research of over 300,000 business executives, LinkedIn reaches more C-level executives (CEO, CFO, COO, etc.) than any other news or business website. And 90% of members say they are involved in purchasing decisions. If you're selling B2B, these are the folks you want to meet, and LinkedIn is the place to meet them.

WHY LINKEDIN IS ESSENTIAL

Kind of like being on Facebook, setting up a LinkedIn profile has become something you just need to do. By this point, if you're a business professional and you're *not* on LinkedIn, people are going to wonder how legitimate you are. If you're a business, you should also create a company page to go along with your personal profile.

Whether you are new to LinkedIn or have been around the block, I would encourage you to sign up for one of our free training sessions at **LinkedWebinar.com**. No matter where you're at on the LinkedIn experience curve, this free training will help you take your game to the next level. In the training, we touch on the basics, but we spend most of our time diving into more advanced LinkedIn strategies. One of the things you'll get when you sign up at **LinkedWebinar.com** is access to additional free training, including how to properly structure and optimize your LinkedIn profile. An effective profile is essential for everything we'll be doing in the rest of this program.

COMMON PRACTICES ON LINKEDIN

The most common way business people used LinkedIn is for an online, up-to-date Rolodex—an enormous, accurate database of professional contacts. Members set up their own profile pages so others can find them and learn about their company, title, skills, work history, etc.

Most LinkedIn users do much more than just set up a profile. They seek out friends and colleagues to form connections. They log on frequently to send messages and to see who has messaged them. And with one of the most popular features, they look to see who has been checking out their profile. People can't seem to resist finding out who's interested enough in them to peruse their profile. In this way, it's a lot like Facebook or any other social network.

There are also more strategic ways people use LinkedIn. A common one is for recruiting employees. LinkedIn is now the number-one tool that recruiters and headhunters use to find staff. A potential employer can view your current position, your employment history, your skills, and see if you know any of the same people. The second way, a mirror of the first, is as a job-seeking tool. LinkedIn is a great way to reach out to potential employers and ask if they are hiring.

But none of these common practices leverage the true potential of this robust business tool.

HARNESSING THE REAL POWER OF LINKEDIN

Now we're getting to the good stuff. What's coming up here

is one of the most powerful ways to use LinkedIn—as a B2B marketing tool to grow your business. This practice includes a number of focused, targeted, and systematic ways to connect with prospects and turn them into sales leads directly on LinkedIn.

First, you can search for and join some of the different LinkedIn groups that have been created around all sorts of subject matter and interests. Whether you're a public accountant, former collegiate athlete, engineering major, food truck operator or plumbing contractor, you can find groups filled with people who have similar interests and backgrounds. If your title is chief technology officer, you can find groups for CTOs and senior-level technology people. If you're in hot tub sales, you can find groups that are all about selling hot tubs.

There are also groups based on geography. So if you work for a chain of clothing stores in Topeka, Kansas, you can find a Topeka retail group. If you are a business out of Australia, you can find groups of other businesses based Down Under.

There are over two million LinkedIn groups. And some of the most popular ones have hundreds of thousands of members. There are even a few with over a million members. Once you're a member, you can post content in these groups and many of the people who are members of the group—whether it's 50 or 50,000—will see that content. This ability to get your content in front of so many people is a super-powerful feature of LinkedIn.

And you can join lots of different groups. Currently, you can be a member of up to fifty groups on LinkedIn. When you're in fifty of the right groups (i.e. the audiences you want to reach) and you have a plan for sharing content into those groups on a regular basis, a tremendous number of interested people will see that content. It's powerful.

In addition to just sharing content into those groups, you can also get involved in discussions in your groups. You can jump in and start conversations of your own, or comment on other people's ongoing discussions. It works kind of like the old school bulletin boards from back in the day, only online and in a group that's already curated around a common interest.

TAKING IT TO THE NEXT LEVEL: CREATING YOUR OWN LINKEDIN GROUP

So you've seen how you can get significant value by simply joining existing groups and sharing your content in them. Now the next-level payoff comes when you start your *own* group.

Do you remember that one of the objectives we started out with was to position yourself as a leader? By creating a LinkedIn group you automatically place yourself as the default leader of that community. When you're running the group, *you* determine who is invited to join, so you can target your top sales prospects. And when you reach out to those people to talk business, they're much more open to you because they view you as a leader in that space.

Another big advantage to creating and leading a LinkedIn group is that you can send out a group email blast or newsletter, called an announcement, once a week. That's basically an email blast to your entire group in which you can say whatever you want. You can use it for promotion. You can use it to share content that's valuable to the group. You can tell people about a webinar you have coming up. You can use it to highlight a case study.

Whatever you want to say, as group leader you have access to the inboxes of everyone in your LinkedIn group. That's a pretty powerful tool and a really nice feature that comes along with running your own group. We'll go deeper into harnessing the power of creating your own LinkedIn group in a later chapter.

But before you launch your own group, you need to spend some time figuring out exactly whom you want in the group. In other words, who are your best sales prospects?

IDENTIFYING YOUR IDEAL PROSPECT

Identifying your ideal prospect is the first step in our process. We call this step "prospect profile development." Essentially this means figuring out who are the decision makers that you're trying to reach, and writing down a description of them. Start with the industries that you are interested in targeting, the geographic areas you want to focus on, in what countries, what cities, and what states. Next, determine what size companies to target.

Pro tip: it's almost never "any size company." Most businesses are going to have some sort of sweet spot that their ideal prospects fall into. Maybe you want to work with businesses that have over five million in sales but less than fifty million, or ones with between fifteen and one hundred employees.

Next up: Decide which types of people within those target companies you want to form relationships with. Who are the actual decision makers? The VP of purchasing or the plant manager? The CFO or the CTO?

Start by looking at your current customers. Note the people who typically do the buying from you, and what positions and titles those people have. For example, if your company supplies cement to the construction industry, the decision makers you deal with from company to company could be the purchasing manager, the project manager, the project foreman, the COO, or even the CEO. Make a list of those different job titles.

Finally, search LinkedIn for the different job titles you just listed. You should find thousands—which is great, because now you know you have plenty of prospects to reach out to. Now narrow them down by the criteria you decided on above: geographic location, company size, etc.

For example, let's say you're looking for shop foremen. Here's the procedure you'd follow:

1. Type "shop foreman" into the top search bar on LinkedIn. You'll see close to 20,000 results.

2. Narrow that search by location—say, shop foremen in Chicago. 473 results.

3. If desired, narrow it down even further—say, shop foremen at Chicago companies that have ten or fewer employees.

4. Repeat this process with any other job titles you want to look for.

YOUR TARGET PROSPECTS SHOULD BE ACTIVE ON LINKEDIN

Next, you want to make sure that the prospects you're targeting look like they're somewhat active on LinkedIn.

What does that look like?

Check to see if a prospect:

- Has a profile picture
- Has more than just a few connections
- Has written a well-developed profile

If a prospect is missing any of those elements, they're probably not all that tuned in to LinkedIn. So don't pursue that prospect—they won't be engaged enough to respond to your messages.

Fortunately this level of non-engagement is relatively rare. Most of the time, we find thousands of highly-engaged prospects to go after—sometimes tens of thousands or even hundreds of thousands.

Pro tip: Launch one campaign at a time. Focus that campaign

on one core type of prospect, especially when you first start. If there are multiple different markets for your product or service, that's great. You can absolutely plan additional campaigns targeted to those other markets. But do it *after* your first campaign is up and running and successful.

For example, say you provide information technology services. The first campaign you do might target the healthcare market. After the success of that first campaign, you could then launch a second campaign targeting insurance companies. The two campaigns would be completely separate because the content, messaging, prospects, and LinkedIn groups are completely different for those two target markets. So trying to do them at the same time divides your efforts and scatters your fire, while doing them in sequence allows you to focus fully on each one.

Remember the wisdom of Ron Swanson: don't half-ass two things, whole-ass one thing.

THE INITIAL DATABASE BUILD

Before you begin your first campaign, narrow down your list to the couple thousand absolute best potential clients for your business. Always aim for the decision makers, the people who can buy your product or service. Keep refining and narrowing your search until you get down to about 2,000 to 3,000 solid prospects.

Once you have your list of prospects, it's time to start reaching out via connection requests. To do this, reach out to each prospect through LinkedIn and invite them to connect with you. These invitations include personal messages between you and the prospect, no one else. So not only does this tactic create a feeling of professional intimacy, it also allows you to customize each message to the prospect.

Include their first name, mention something you admire about their business, a mutual LinkedIn connection or something you have in common, and ask to connect with their LinkedIn profile. Make sure you set aside enough time to give each message its own personal touch. Because these messages are personally customized and you're only asking them for a connection (do *not* try to sell them anything in this initial message!), the acceptance rate is usually pretty high, often between 50–75%.

So even though these are cold prospects who don't know you, more than half will usually accept that connection request from you. And just like that, you now have a database of strong potential clients to start working through the process.

MESSAGING CAMPAIGNS

Once you've done your initial database build, it's time to begin a personal messaging campaign.

Start by sending a few friendly messages—nothing about your business, no selling, just connecting and sharing things that might interest them. Keep them informal, use your own words, and be genuine. For example:

Message 1: "Hey, Mark, thanks for connecting. Congrats on your success."

Message 2: "I came across this article the other day. I really thought you might be into it. Would really love to hear your thoughts."

Message 3: "There's a discussion going on in my LinkedIn group right now on [subject the prospect works with or has interest in]. I bet you'd have some great insights to share. Here's the link if you're interested. "

(Repeat and vary messages 2 and 3 as often as desired—the idea is to share lots of valuable content with the prospect while keeping your name in front of them.)

Message 4: "Hey Mark, we've been touching base here on LinkedIn for a while. It'd be great to learn more about your business. Do you have time for a call next Thursday any time between 10 a.m. and noon?"

Note that the first three message types are all about building a relationship with the prospect. They are consistent but not eager, friendly but not flattering, personal but not sales-y, and professional but not formal. They feel like a casual note a friend would send, not a warm-up to a sales pitch.

The genius of messages like these is that even though you're sending out hundreds of them, maybe even thousands, in a campaign, each one reads like you're only sending it to one person. This is why making each one personal is so important.

No one will respond well to a message that looks like you've sent the same message to 200 other people and just changed the salutation. But almost anyone will respond well to a message that reads like a letter written just to them.

But won't this take a ton of time?

In a word: yes. Because the messages are all personalized and there is no way to automate the process, there is legwork involved. All these one-on-one messages have to be sent manually and individually. But that's why it works so well! Because it takes effort and time to execute, most people aren't willing to do it. And that's how you're going to stand out.

Again, there is no way to automate this part of the process. You or someone on your team will need to sit at the computer and send several hundred messages to the prospects in the messaging campaign. It's going to take some time; typically an hour for every couple hundred messages. (As the CEO of your company, you will not want to do this entire project yourself. Design and oversee it, yes. Do all the writing, no.)

Fortunately, there are two important factors that make it absolutely worth putting in that time.

First, you don't have to do this all at once. In fact, you absolutely shouldn't—receiving all four of the above messages within a month, let alone a week, will put a prospect's guard up and make them wonder if they're being set up for a sales pitch.

Remember the schedule we discussed earlier. For each prospect, the path from message one to message four should take between two and three months. That's one message every three weeks or so. If you want to accelerate things, we recommend going no faster than every two weeks. Over several hundred prospects, that's still a lot of messages to send, but now the workload is spread out over a much more manageable timeframe.

Second, many people just don't have the discipline to do this. Because it can be such tedious work, very few people bother to do it all. So when you do put in the discipline and time to do it, you automatically stand out. You're the 1% who's done what the other 99% wouldn't do. So while your prospects are receiving and forgetting dozens of sales pitches from your undisciplined competitors, they'll remember the effort you made to genuinely connect with them—and jump at the chance to get on the phone with you.

I'm not including the exact instructions, clicks and screenshots to set up a messaging campaign and send messages here, for a couple reasons. One, because LinkedIn is very intuitive and easy to use. If you can use Facebook, you can set up your own group and send messages on LinkedIn. Two, each business requires a different approach.

Within our training program, Linked University, we include detailed instructions on setting up and executing your messaging campaigns, including scripts for each message. But even with that, we highly recommend that you don't use these scripts verbatim. To get the best results, you really should put them into your own words and craft these messages so they speak to YOUR prospects. If you find you're struggling with any aspect of how to set these messages up, I'd highly encourage you to join our advanced training program Linked University.

KEEP TRACK OF EVERYTHING

It is essential that you keep track of these messaging campaigns. You need to be able to tell at a glance whom you have reached out to, with which message, and when and how to follow up with them. When you've got a couple thousand people in your campaign, it's super easy to lose track and get disorganized very quickly. Once this happens, getting back on track will be almost impossible. So don't let it happen!

Here is a link (**LinkedSelling.com/Tracking**) to an Excel spreadsheet that we use as a tracking form. It's a simple spreadsheet that shows how we structure and organize all these messages. The spreadsheet gives you real-time access to the data of all the prospects in the campaign, all the relevant information about those people, what parts of the campaign they're currently in, what messages they've received, and which messages they're queued up to receive.

This will make tracking the campaign simple. It's intuitive and easy to use for this process so that you have a one-stop shop to go in and see everything going on in the campaign. If you want to customize the spreadsheet you can easily create your own. Or, if you have a CRM system that you think would do the trick, great! No matter how you want to organize the data, the key is that you do it. We'll dig a lot deeper into creating your own tracking system in Chapter 7.

After you've built your prospect list and started running your messaging campaign, it's time to launch your own group. We'll get back to this in Chapter 7 to show you the method we've found is most effective, but first take a look at this case study to see what kind of results are in store if you stick to this program.

Cohen Architectural Woodworking:
$10 Million in Revenue Growth

How do you go from being an old-school regional supplier to the construction industry to one that closes long-term, multi-million dollar contracts with international corporations? Cohen Architectural Woodworking (CAW) was hungry to answer that question. And the way they achieved it was certainly *not* by doing more of the same old-fashioned sales and marketing grind.

In business since 1975, the Cohen family has maintained a phenomenal reputation among its client base. But historically most of these clients only placed occasional orders for special projects. While many of these were large projects and quite profitable, the seemingly never-ending revenue roller coaster that comes along with being a "job shop" just wasn't working long-term.

Instead, CAW wanted to upgrade. Their new goal was to focus almost exclusively on national accounts—major corporate clients that would name CAW as the single-source vendor for all their new and remodel construction projects. The only problem was that the traditional ways of selling just weren't generating results. CAW's sales team wasn't getting in the door to forge the relationships with the buyers and key decision makers in the construction management departments.

Realizing that the old ways weren't working, the Cohen management team turned to us at LinkedSelling. Even though all this LinkedIn marketing stuff seemed a bit foreign to them, they believed our system could deliver a scalable campaign to reach these high-end corporate decision makers. And after we worked them through a systematic relationship building process, a large percentage of their highest-level prospects were happy to schedule a call.

For Cohen Architectural Woodworking, we achieved this in two ways. First, we built and quickly grew a LinkedIn group catering to their ideal prospects. Not a group about woodworking, but an industry-focused group that their *prospects* would actually enjoy and care about. The group has since grown to over 15,000 members!

The LinkedIn group regularly keeps the CAW name in front of thousands of prospects. They see the group leader, Ben Cohen, VP of sales, and CAW as leaders in the space. The top-of-mind awareness it has built for CAW is massive.

Second, we developed several thousand direct connections (highly-targeted prospects) via Ben Cohen's LinkedIn account. For these first-degree connections, we exposed them to daily status updates and other communications, most importantly our lead generation messaging campaigns.

Working the most high-value prospects through personal messaging campaigns results in a steady stream of sales opportunities. Some of these conversations result in quick sales orders, while some are more introductory. But either way, the value of getting a foot in the door with that many qualified prospects is huge.

Over time, we nurture both of these databases (the LinkedIn group + the direct connections) to position CAW as one of the good guys—*not* pushy salespeople always talking about themselves, but sharers of relevant and balanced content that isn't intrusive or annoying. That's why, after working prospects through the system, approximately 29% agree to a phone call. That's huge.

But what kind of manpower did Cohen have to allocate to the management of this campaign? Since they hired us to run the campaign for them, it only took about two hours per month of coordination with their LinkedSelling Account Manager, plus the time needed to schedule and field sales calls with prospects who wanted to talk. The entire campaign is managed by our team. We literally take it all the way to the point where prospects agree to a phone call and then hand it off to CAW.

To date, our LinkedSelling campaign has generated more than $10 million in new revenue for CAW. Furthermore, the campaign has positioned CAW as a leader in the industry, and maintained a top-of-mind campaign in front of thousands of prospects. Needless to say, CAW executives have been ecstatic with the results, and the campaign continues to this day.

LEAD YOUR PACK

There are two primary ways we build relationships with your prospects on LinkedIn. In Chapter 4 we talked about the first one, personal messaging campaigns. In this chapter we'll dig into the other one, creating and leading your own LinkedIn group.

Let's start with an example.

A lawyer I know who concentrates on building and construction law created a professional LinkedIn group called The Saint Louis Contractor Referral Network. As the founder and president of the group, he invites key executives from the industry to join the network, and he organizes conferences, panel discussions, keynote speakers, and social events. He sends out mailings, contacts executives about speaking on panels, and introduces the keynote speakers at those panels.

By doing these things he has established himself as a respected authority and well-known leader in the industry—even though he's probably never operated a cement mixer or driven a dump truck. So when a building or construction executive in the Contractor Referral Network needs a lawyer, guess who they think of first? Conversely, when the lawyer calls a construction executive and asks for a meeting, they usually say yes. They seem him as a peer and a real player in the industry.

LinkedIn allows you to do exactly what the Saint Louis Contractor Referral Network does, but online. As the founder and creator of the group, you will control who joins, you will share content with members, and you will be the leader of all group initiatives. Creating and running your own LinkedIn group positions you as a leader in that industry, space, market, or geographic region where you do business. The value of being seen as the leader of a group of high-level business professionals cannot be overstated.

There are many ways to establish yourself as an authority in your field of business, but most of them are either very expensive, or very difficult, or both. Let's take a look at some of the typical or traditional ways you might go about it:

- Write a bestselling book on your industry. Not easy.

- Market yourself as a keynote speaker for industry conferences and conventions. Difficult and potentially expensive.

- Hire a public relations firm to get your name mentioned in newspapers and magazines. Expensive.

- Write a hundred articles and pitch yourself to become a featured columnist in your industry's trade publications. Not easy.

- Organize and run an annual conference. Expensive and difficult.

What's more, none of these ways guarantee the result of being seen as an industry leader for more than a little while—if they even work to begin with. So if none of these tactics are the best way to become an industry leader, what *is* the best way?

LINKEDIN LEADERSHIP

The great thing about creating and leading your own LinkedIn group is that you can do it very systematically, in your free time (or even delegate the heavy lifting to somebody on your team), and at comparatively low cost. Imagine how much time, effort, and expense would be involved in launching a new industry conference, or writing a bestselling book. Or paying travel expenses to fly all over the country giving lectures and seminars. (Not to mention the risk that these strategies might flop. The book may never find a publisher. The conference might never catch on.)

In contrast, on day one of founding your LinkedIn group you have already positioned yourself as a leader in that space, and on day two your prospects will begin to see you as an authority—all because you are the founder and leader of the community.

Here's another example. A client of ours runs a payment processing business. He tries to sell companies on letting his firm process all their credit card transactions. So he started a LinkedIn group that focuses on wholesalers and distributors from California. He invited mostly CFOs and CEOs of large wholesalers and distributors to join the group. On day one, he was seen as a leader in this space—even though he had never run a wholesale or distribution company in his life. To be honest, he's not even *in that industry*. He's in the payment processing business. But he knew enough about the wholesale and distribution business to find and share pertinent content with the members, and lead the group discussions. The group now has a constantly-growing membership of targeted executives that our client is looking to do business with, and they all know who the group leader is.

LinkedIn groups are a highly efficient, cost-effective way to reach out to the key prospects in your target market from a position of strength and authority. And when you approach the C-level executives who are your prospects as a *peer*, on their level, you'll have much greater success.

WHO SHOULD BE THE LEADER?

Since the end result of this process is more sales leads, some companies consider having a salesperson or a sales manager be the one to create and lead the LinkedIn group. This tactic almost never works.

Why?

Because of the idea of peerage.

A peer is someone working at the same level as you. In Britain, "the peerage" refers to a social class where all members are at the same level of nobility. And we all know how powerful "peer pressure" can be when people at our own level ask us to join them.

The leader of a LinkedIn group will be approaching high-level decision makers and buyers. But those prospects will be most open to approaches *from their own peers*. A CEO or CFO at a prospect company is going to view your company founder or CFO as a peer. So if a lower-level sales rep contacts the CEO, then the CEO is likely to think the sales rep is just trying to sell him something.

Now that doesn't mean that your CEO or founder will necessarily run the group! But all of it will be done from the CEO's LinkedIn page, or that of an equivalent peer.

RESEARCH EXISTING GROUPS

Before launching your group, do a search to see what other groups are out there and how similar they are to yours. Of course, you can't use the same title as an existing group. But even if there are groups very similar to yours, you can still launch a new group into that same space. In fact, the existence of similar groups shows that there's an audience for you to tap into!

It's just like deciding to launch a new blog into a crowded

marketplace, like a new travel blog, for example. If you've got something to say, and a unique position or spin, then there's room for your blog too.

Same goes for LinkedIn groups. Even if you find a group that's exactly like the one you want to create, it's unlikely that all the people in the industry are in that group. And just because they are in *that* group doesn't mean they won't also join *your* group. There is plenty of room for more groups, especially groups where the leader is actively engaged in sharing great content.

Be sure to position your group as exclusive, and for high-level people. The name of your group should communicate exclusivity and seniority. If there is already a group called "Reality Television Professionals," launch your group and title it something like "Reality Television Executive Leadership Network." It's a subtle difference, but look at how much more powerful the second group name sounds.

INVITING PROSPECTS TO JOIN YOUR GROUP

In the previous chapter we talked about how to do a database build by reaching out to about 1,500 prospects via personal one-on-one connection requests. Once that database of first-degree connections grows to a decent size, somewhere between 300 and 500 prospects, you're ready to launch a group.

Now reach out to those prospects through another personal message and invite them to join your group. We typically see a couple hundred of them join the group off of that initial invitation. As you keep marketing your group, it should grow by at least a couple hundred members every month. Your goal will be to grow it to several thousand members. And the bigger the group becomes, the more momentum it has to keep growing—eventually it will basically market itself and grow on its own.

By this point you will have two databases: the LinkedIn group, and your first-degree connections. There will likely be overlap between the two—some people will agree to connect with you, others will join the group, and some will do both. (Yes, some also won't do either. But if you have both to offer them, you're going to increase the chances that they will at least do one!)

KEEP PROMOTING AND GROWING YOUR GROUP

One of the best ways to grow your group is by visiting other, similar groups for your industry, or any groups that your prospects are likely to belong. Then message the members of that other group and invite them to join your group. For example, if the group you launched is "The Chicago Banking Forum," you may want to visit groups like "Chicago Finance Executives" or "The Chicago Financial Forum."

In addition to personal one-on-one invitations, there are a number of ways you can continuously grow your LinkedIn group, including:

- Sharing content from the group with your email list.
- Promoting the group on your other social media properties.
- Promoting the group on your website.

- Regularly posting status updates on LinkedIn about your group.
- Sharing discussions from your group in other LinkedIn groups.
- Running LinkedIn ads to promote your group.
- Negotiating partnerships with other group owners to promote your group.

Okay, now that you have all these awesome prospects in your group, what do you do with them? How do you strategically form relationships with them? And more importantly, how do you make the group worth their time? In the next chapter we'll show you *how* to lead your pack. But first, check out the case study below. The Swip Systems story is a great example of how it all comes together.

· · · · · · CASE STUDY · · · · · ·

Swip Systems
Return on Investment: 447%

Swip Systems is a technology company based in Illinois. Their services include software and mobile development, infrastructure, cloud solutions, automation, and intelligence. The landscape of the IT industry is crowded and competition is fierce. Swip needed a way to stand out from the pack and be seen as a premium solutions provider.

Our system allowed founder and CEO Tom Swip to position himself as a peer to the senior C-level decision makers he targets—the CEO, CFO, and CTO. To reach these prospects, we first created and promoted a LinkedIn group called Midwest Manufacturing Leaders, with Tom Swip as the leader of the group. We targeted only senior-level manufacturing executives who had the power to make key buying decisions. The group has since grown to more than 5,000 members. Second, we developed several thousand direct connections via Tom Swip's LinkedIn account. We send these connections regular communications and updates, constantly staying in front of them and building brand awareness of Swip Systems.

As always, we position relevant and balanced content in front of prospects in a way that isn't intrusive or annoying. That's why, after working prospects through the system, again, approximately 29% agree to a phone call. Swip Systems then plugged those leads into their existing sales process, and converted a percentage of them to paying clients.

The results?

- Number of prospects in funnel: 6,557 and counting.
- Positioned the Swip Systems brand as a prestige service provider in the manufacturing systems industry.
- Maintained a top-of-mind campaign in front of thousands of high-value prospects.
- Generating a steady stream of leads and calls with highly-targeted prospects.
- ROI on investment with LinkedSelling: Over $600,000 in new business.

As an added bonus, the LinkedIn group and campaign has been so effective that Swip Systems has now taken it into the real world. We're currently working with them to host a quarterly Midwest Manufacturing Leaders in-person event and conference.

SIX

BUILD RELATIONSHIPS BY SHARING VALUE

Now that you've created two large databases of potential customers, what's the best way to earn their trust and eventually earn the right to ask them for a call or a sales meeting?

We've talked about it a little already.

In a word, it's *value*.

The key to building relationships with your prospects is to add value to their world. How? By giving them meaningful, useful information that can help them in *their* business.

You can't add value to your potential customers by aggressively pestering them to buy your products. That will just annoy them and make them regret connecting with you on LinkedIn. Instead, go out and find information that is both timely and helpful to your potential customers—and then share that info with them without asking for anything in return.

In this chapter I'll show you how to set up a systematic plan for finding and sharing that content. We'll talk about some software tools that will help you automate the process to make it even easier. And I'll give you a few strategies to encourage discussions and activity in your LinkedIn group.

WHAT CONTENT TO SHARE

How will you know what content will appeal to your target customers? Cat pictures and BuzzFeed quizzes aren't going to cut it for this kind of connection. Fortunately there's a very simple rule for determining what content to use—and it's one you'll recognize if you've ever taken a public speaking class.

Know your audience.

The better you know your potential customers—and their industry—the better you'll be able to recognize what type of information they will find helpful. So use that knowledge to post and share content that they will truly care about.

Ask yourself: What do my potential customers care about, what challenges do they face, what do they worry about, what makes their lives easier, and what's important to their business?

If your business sells electrical supplies and you have twenty years experience calling on customers in the industry, you probably have a clear picture of who they are and what matters to them. So if you've built a LinkedIn group of independent electrical contractors, it's a good bet they care about issues like:

- Preparing competitive bids
- Dealing with labor union issues
- Recruiting qualified apprentices
- Staying in line with ever-changing government regulations
- New electrical technologies
- Product recalls
- Maintaining a fleet of vehicles
- Cutting costs on wiring
- Preventing copper theft
- Fire and safety codes
- Trends in interior design and lighting
- Dispatch and scheduling efficiency
- Economic data, like construction figures and new housing starts
- And many more topics along these lines

If you post useful content about these topics to a LinkedIn group full of electrical contractors, they will love you.

See, these people really need to know this stuff, but they don't always have time to look for it themselves. All the information you'll share with them is already out there somewhere, sure, but it's not aggregated, curated, or all in one place. They'd have to spend a few hours every day searching the Internet for it.

That's where you come in. Using the automation tools in this chapter you'll streamline and automate the information aggregation, curation, and sharing process, so your prospects won't have to spend hours digging to find this information (and neither will you). Before long these potential customers will consider you to be some sort of industry guru—or at least a very helpful person who really understands their business.

While you're thinking about that, think about this.

Everyone in your LinkedIn group of independent electrical contractors will know that you sell electrical supplies. You won't make any secret of that—it's your business and you're proud of it. But even though you sell supplies your group members could use, you rarely, if ever, ask them to buy anything. You don't post about your own business and products at all.

So when you regularly post helpful articles about the industry *without* trying to sell anything, you look like a hero, not to mention a super-knowledgeable industry leader. Over time, your potential customers will gradually come to view you as a trusted resource for their business. And when they need a new electrical supplier, guess whose name will be first on their call list?

Okay, that's great for people who know their potential customers inside and out, but what if you *don't* know the industry all that well? For example, you might be a CPA firm that spent the last ten years specializing in auditing hospitals, but now you want to expand into the construction business. How do you handle that?

Actually, you'll do exactly the same thing as when you do know the industry—you'll just need to do more research ahead of time. Talk to some of your potential customers in the target industry. Take them to lunch. Get to know them. Ask them about the state of their industry, what's going well, and what challenges are on the horizon. What are their concerns? What government regulations do they struggle with? What's it going to take to have a great year?

Don't have time for lunches? You can shortcut the process by reviewing the discussions happening in online forums or other LinkedIn groups. With an hour or two of research, you'll uncover the hot topics that your target market is really keyed in on. Once you figure out which information and topics will resonate with your group, it's just a matter of doing a little Googling to find your sources.

FINDING AND ORGANIZING YOUR CONTENT

In an hour of searching the Internet you will be able to find industry websites, trade publications, and blogs that focus on the content your prospects are interested in. Save these links in your bookmarks.

Then find some of the leading experts, opinion leaders, or speakers in your industry and visit their websites. If they don't have websites, look for articles they've written or talks they've given. Bookmark all of those links too.

Next, set up some Google alerts based on keywords and topics that you've identified as important to your prospects. This way, anytime a new article or post on any of them goes up, you'll get a notification so you won't miss it.

Keep in mind—to continue our electrical supply example above—you won't just be looking for electrician and electrical industry websites. You'll be finding websites and blogs about other topics too, like unions, interior design, lighting and ceiling fixtures, fire safety, economic data on construction, maintaining fleets of vehicles, scheduling and efficiency, energy conservation, management, accounting, marketing, and so on. Get as broad—and as specific—as you can.

So once you collect all these sources, there's an easy way to organize them using a feed aggregator—I recommend Feedly. The term "aggregator" sounds intimidating, but it's really simple. You sign up for a free Feedly account at **Feedly.com**, and dump in all of your website addresses. Then instead of taking the time to visit all of those sites every week, you just go to your Feedly every few days, review the fire hose of content that's accumulated there, and pick out the best stuff to share. Keep a spreadsheet of which content you shared and when, so you can keep track of it and not post the same content twice.

POSTING CONTENT

Ideally, you'll want to post new content pretty much every

day. You can even post twice a day if you're so inspired. If you have Feedly set up with enough different sources there should be plenty of content to allow you to share something daily.

To keep from overwhelming yourself or your marketing team, you definitely want to automate this posting process. We recommend a program called Oktopost [LinkedUniversity.com/Oktopost]. With Oktopost you can automate the distribution of your content right into LinkedIn. And while it does not currently share into groups, it's the best tool for automating all of your daily status updates. Follow that link above and you'll get a free trial of Oktopost so you can check it out.

Oktopost integrates seamlessly with LinkedIn, so your content looks just like you posted it manually—it doesn't look like an automated program did it. Even better, you can put your content delivery on autopilot by scheduling it weeks or months in advance. So if you're going to Maui for vacation, it will keep posting content while you're away, so it looks like you're at your desk instead of on the golf course. Even if you're just doing regular daily work, Oktopost takes the task of daily posting off your to-do list.

STIMULATE GROUP ACTIVITY

In the early days after the formation of your group, don't be discouraged if it's not bustling with activity. Building momentum and activity within the group takes time. But as your numbers grow to a few hundred or more, the amount of posting and discussions will also increase. The best and most successful LinkedIn groups are vibrant places where many people engage in posting content and discussing topics. So you want to encourage others to be active in your group. There are two effective ways to do this.

The first way to get others to actively participate in your group is to go recruit members who are active and vocal in *other* groups. If someone is active and engaged in a different group, they will probably bring a lot of life to your group as well.

The second way to build participation and engagement in your group is by discussion promotion. Instead of posting an article, or a resource, or a case study, you just post a question to the entire group. For example, "Hey, what are the things that you're planning to do next year to grow your business?" To make sure the discussion gets going, message about thirty or forty group members and ask them to weigh in. "Hey, Linda, I posted a discussion question in the group. I know you have big things planned for this year and I'd love to hear your thoughts. If you'd leave a comment, that would be awesome." Usually when a few people start commenting, that's all it takes for the discussion to take off.

Pro tip: This technique works best when there are already a hundred or so people in your group. The fewer people in the group, the more messaging you'll need to do to get the discussion going. But once your group grows to 500 or more, discussions tend to take off on their own and active promotion is usually no longer necessary.

Once the group starts to come to life, human nature will kick in and the group will become even more popular. People want to be a part of something that's happening and vibrant. No one wants to join a ghost town. So you'll have to work a little harder initially to stir up activity until the group grows big enough to take on a life of its own. Once it does, you'll be amazed at the number of *inbound* connection requests you'll be receiving as the leader of the group. When you position yourself as the leader of an active group and an authority in the space, people will want to connect with you and join the group.

KEEP GROWING THE GROUP

As the group members get in the habit of posting content and participating in discussions, the group will organically grow. But as the leader, it's your job to help that growth along. So until the group starts growing faster than you can send invitations, definitely keep sending direct connection requests inviting others to join. This not only helps fuel the group but also allows you to continue reaching out to really targeted prospects.

It's important to point out one thing: Initially, you grew the group by inviting your connections. So you might be thinking, why not just continue sending connection requests first, and then inviting those new connections to join the group? Because there is a limitation that LinkedIn places on direct connection requests.

You can have no more than 5,000 connection requests per person. At some point you may bump up against that. Which means that you need to carefully craft your messaging when approaching new prospects via a connection request. The better your hit rate, the more runway you'll have. This limit only applies to direct connection requests, though. If you do hit this limit, congratulations! You'll likely have some pretty awesome results on your hands. And it's easy to turn to other strategies to reach new prospects, to continue developing new connections and leads. Or, consider utilizing another profile from a colleague in your office.

MORE PROSPECTS THAN YOU CAN HANDLE

By posting great content, promoting discussions, and continuing to grow your group, you will regularly boost the number of warm leads you're generating for your business. These strategies will grow your connections in a really targeted way, and most of the people connecting with you are going to be a good fit with your prospect profile. Many of our clients who use this system find it challenging to keep up with the flow of new prospects! What a great problem to have!

The sales pipeline can be viewed as a funnel. Using the tactics described above helps create a constant flow of new prospects pouring into the top of the funnel. If you do this consistently you'll have a predictable stream of warm leads coming through every month. You can literally run these campaigns and groups for years.

What to do with all these prospects? After a few months of this flow, you may have more than you have time to connect with!

Of course, you could hire more staff to handle the overflow, but before you call your HR department, try this:

Go through all the prospects in your group, and pick the very best ones, the ones you're practically salivating to work with. Start working those through a targeted messaging campaign, the kind we talked about in Chapter 4. After a couple months of messaging, you send them Message 4 and request a phone call. As we've seen, on average 29% of those prospects agree (compared to a measly 1–2% without the relationship-building work).

And there's an added bonus. Every once in a while people in your group will reach out to *you* and say, "Hey, I'm in the market for what you sell. Would you like to talk?" And you didn't even need to do any extra work for that to happen!

Louder Online: 384% Return on Investment

Aaron Agius runs one of Australia's leading marketing consultancies, Louder Online. The firm specializes in search, social, and content marketing. When Aaron approached us in the summer of 2012, he was looking for a strategy to not just generate more business, but to also position his company as *the* leader in his space.

CHALLENGE MEETS OPPORTUNITY

The challenge for Aaron's business is pretty simple. As with many consulting firms (and especially marketing firms), the competitive landscape is crowded. There are literally thousands of other marketing agencies competing for the same business. And some of them are pretty aggressive in their tactics.

On LinkedIn, that aggressiveness really poisons the well. SEO and marketing service providers are hammering their prospects with messages on LinkedIn. Naturally, these prospects quickly tune out all these overt sales pitches.

But believe it or not, that aggressive environment actually *helps* Aaron. For Louder Online we brought the tools and experience to cut through this toxic perception and position Aaron as a *peer* to the senior marketing decision makers he targets.

THE TARGET MARKET

Aaron's company isn't looking to work with mom-and-pop operations. They have big-ticket engagements and work with Australia's largest brands. The people he targets within these companies are often digital marketing managers, marketing directors, CMOs, etc. These kinds of people aren't easily sold just because you sent them a message on LinkedIn.

To reach these high-level prospects, we knew we needed a unique approach to stand above the crowd. An approach that would position Aaron as a true leader in his space, keep his name consistently in front of his best prospects (in a non-spammy way), and make his presence so rock-solid that his prospects would jump at joining his community and (eventually) doing business with him.

THE CAMPAIGN STRUCTURE

When we position our clients as leaders in their space, and position them in front of literally thousands of prospects over and over again, the response rate when we go for a phone call or other "call to action" averages 29%. These are prospects who, taking the old-fashioned approach, wouldn't give you the time of day. But when we work them through a systematic relationship-building process, 29% will be happy to schedule a call.

For Aaron and Louder Online, we achieved this in two ways. First, we built and quickly grew a LinkedIn group catering to their best prospects. Not a group about the services that Louder provides—SEO and inbound marketing—but rather an industry focused group that their *prospects* would actually enjoy, care about enough to join, and stay engaged in for a long time.

The group has grown from zero to over 6,000 members.

The LinkedIn group allows us to keep Aaron's name in front of thousands of prospects for the long term. They see him and Louder Online as leaders in the marketing arena. Furthermore, the discussions cultivated within the group allow Aaron to directly engage with potential clients.

Additionally, we developed several thousand direct connections with highly-targeted prospects via Aaron's LinkedIn account. For these direct-messaging connections, we communicate with them via frequent updates and content sharing so that Louder Online is always top-of-mind.

WHAT ARE THE RESULTS?

- Number of prospects in funnel: 8,505 and counting.
- Positioned the Louder Online brand as a leader in their market.
- Maintained a top-of-mind campaign in front of thousands of prospects.
- Generating a steady stream of leads and calls with highly-targeted prospects.
- ROI on investment with LinkedSelling: 384%

SEVEN

CREATING YOUR CAMPAIGN TRACKING SYSTEM

Okay, here's a question for you: when we talked about tracking your campaign data back in Chapter 4, did you roll your eyes?

Yeah, that's what I thought.

It's pretty rare to hear someone say that tracking and logging data is their favorite activity.

But here's the thing: Just because it's boring and tedious doesn't mean it isn't important. And being able to track multiple chunks of data throughout your campaigns is going to be critical for your success.

So ignore (or fight off) the urge to be lazy, and take pride in doing the tough stuff! I promise it's going to make your campaigns awesome. Here's why:

Without tracking your activity you are essentially flying aimlessly in the wind. It will be nearly impossible to make any improvements if you can't tell what you have done already. You also need to get a clear picture of what your results look like when you finish different portions of your campaign. And of course, if your results don't turn out the way you expected, the data you tracked will help you know what to adjust.

Fortunately, setting up a tracking system is actually very easy. All you need, as I mentioned in Chapter 4, is a tracking sheet. And while the data in this sheet may become pretty complex as you add to it and customize it, the sheet itself is very simple.

All you need to start is a basic spreadsheet in Excel or Google Docs.

Not only are these sheets simple, they are also hugely customizable. And customization is the most important factor of tracking. What you need to track may not be the same thing that someone else needs to track. Your business and your campaigns are unique to you—you need a tracking sheet that you can design and adapt specifically for them. So as you read through the example, be advised that it's not one size fits all. If your sheet needs to change to meet your campaign needs, make the change.

Most tracking sheets are going to be divided into two parts, contact info and touch point info. On the contacts side you are going to have the basic information: "First Name," "Last Name," "Title," "Company," and "Email Address." That's essentially all LinkedIn will allow you to export for your contacts, and for many that may be all you need. For others you may also need to take note of things like their location, the division each contact works in, or what systems/products/services their company uses. If any other item is important to you, add it to your sheet.

Even though there are no rules as to how your tracking sheet needs to work, it's probably best to build your sheet from left to right instead of top to bottom.

FIRST NAME	LAST NAME	COMPANY	TITLE	EMAIL

So far this stuff is pretty basic. Most people are familiar with setting up spreadsheets of data for prospects. But now it's time to take your sheet one step further and start giving it some moving parts.

Let's say that you are going to run a five-message messaging campaign, meaning you will send five separate messages, each creating a touch point between you and your prospect, and culminating with some call to action. Then you'll want to set up a section of columns that looks like this:

MESSAGE 1	MESSAGE 2	MESSAGE 3	MESSAGE 4	MESSAGE 5

As you add additional campaigns, you can put in additional campaign sections further to the right.

As you set up these messaging campaigns, make sure to include the dates in which your prospects should be receiving messages—both the ones they've already received and the ones going out to them soon. You could even do this in the same area that you have your playbook tracked. Then group the playbook under one heading for the campaign:

M1 1/1/15	M2 1/22/15	M3 2/12/15	M4 3/5/15	M5 3/26/15

Each campaign represents a unique batch of prospects that are running through a particular campaign. Since you are running these campaigns to multiple batches of people at a time, then you will have multiple campaigns running at a time:

CAMPAIGN 1				
M1 1/1/15	M2 1/22/15	M3 2/12/15	M4 3/5/15	M5 3/26/15

CAMPAIGN 2				
M1 1/22/15	M2 2/12/15	M3 3/5/15	M4 3/26/15	M5 4/26/15

Combine your "touch point" section with your "contact" section and you may have something that looks like this (opposite page):

CONTACT INFO					CAMPAIGN 1					CAMPAIGN 2				
FIRST NAME	LAST NAME	COMPANY	TITLE	EMAIL	M1 1/1/15	M2 1/22/15	M3 2/12/15	M4 3/5/15	M5 3/26/15	M1 1/22/15	M2 2/12/15	M3 3/5/15	M4 3/26/15	M5 4/26/15
BOB	SMITH	ABC INC.	OWNER	BOB@ABC.COM	X	X	X	O	O					
TIM	STACK	123.COM	CEO	TIM@123.COM						X	X	O	O	O

You can see now how quickly your tracking sheet can become complex. Hundreds of prospects with many rows and columns of data, with dozens of messaging campaigns going on; it can get hairy pretty quickly. The x's represent messages that have been sent. The q's represent messages that are going to be sent (in the queue).

If this chapter is giving you heart palpitations, then take a deep breath and slow down. You can get started with some very basic columns of data and just take things slow. It will also help to start your messaging campaigns with small batches of prospects at a time, say eight to fifteen per week at most. Once you've mastered tracking a batch that size, you can start sending out larger batches.

At this point you might be wondering, "Josh, that's all fine and dandy, but why go to all this trouble to track this data outside of LinkedIn? Why not stay in their platform?" That's a great question, and unfortunately the answer is that there's no way to give you a great snapshot, in one place, of all your activity on LinkedIn. You absolutely must do it externally.

Anyway, once the sheet is set up, you can look through it for any specific info you need. Want to see how many people have agreed to a phone call? Create a lead column and sort the column with a filter. Want to see how many people are in your third messaging campaign? Sort the Campaign 3, Message 1 column with a filter. Want to see how many people you are connected to at a specific company? Sort the Company column with a filter.

Not only can you see "big picture" data in the campaign, but you can also focus in on each individual prospect to see what they have been exposed to. Then when it's time for a call with one of your prospects, you're not digging around for 30 minutes; all the info is right there in the tracking sheet, so you won't need to search all over LinkedIn to find it.

Pro tip: Periodically you'll want to add new connections to your tracking sheet from LinkedIn. You might think this would be an easy process, but it's actually a little tricky. See, when you want to export contacts from LinkedIn to a spreadsheet, you can't pick and choose which contacts you export. You have to export *all* of them. So when you do a new export after adding several hundred new contacts, you'll need to de-duplicate (remove duplicates from) the spreadsheet before you proceed.

Now, if you are one of those people who are still recovering from those heart palpitations a moment ago, there is good news! Below is a link you can go to if you want to check out an example of a fully-built tracking sheet. It's been customized and has a few other columns of data that are extremely useful to have when running these campaigns. One of those rows is a place for messaging links. If you know you are going to message batches and batches of candidates over and over again, it helps to track a link that sends you straight to a message window for each prospect, instead of having to manually search for them over and over again in LinkedIn. There are also detailed instructions in the sheet on how to de-duplicate lists of contacts.

You can check out the tracking sheet here: LinkedSelling.com/Tracking

Heart palpitations subsiding yet? They should be, because this is not as bad as it seems—and as we talked about at the beginning of this chapter, data is a good thing. It's important to have a handle on how to create a campaign and create a system to track activity and results. Once you can do that, then you have the ability to set up and test an infinite number of different types of messaging campaigns—and know which ones worked the best.

Now that we've looked at tracking your group activity and messaging campaigns, it's time to dig into another powerful tool for demonstrating your expertise and establishing you as a leader in your space: the webinar. Webinars help educate prospects in a totally different way than LinkedIn campaigns do, allowing you as the leader to go much deeper into a subject your audience really wants to know more about. If you do it right, your prospects will see your webinar as another form of valuable content from you. And webinars integrate well into the rest of the system. I'll show you how to maximize the power of webinars in the next chapter.

EIGHT

SUPERPOWER YOUR LINKEDIN CAMPAIGN WITH WEBINARS

Wait...webinars? I thought this was a book about LinkedIn?

It is. But in a broader sense, this is a book about helping you grow a lead generation machine. For my business, we've tripled our revenue each of the last three years. And a big driver for this growth has been the success we've had with webinars. Currently we average about 10,000 webinar registrants per month, mostly on autopilot.

Our playbook to achieve this growth has been a combination of LinkedIn and webinars. So I would be remiss not to show you how you can do the same for your business.

Let's start from the beginning. What is a webinar?

Webinars combine "web" and "seminar" to create a live online lesson or class that hundreds of people can watch simultaneously. Webinars are powerful tools that can boost your credibility and leadership status within your industry, sell products directly, and very effectively generate red-hot sales leads for your business. In this chapter I'll show you how webinars work, why they work, and how to create your own webinar campaign to support your LinkedIn marketing efforts.

WHY WEBINARS?

A knowledgeable speaker giving a well-researched PowerPoint presentation to a live audience is powerful. Public speaking is an excellent business development tool, and it does wonders for your credibility and status in your industry. Unfortunately, public speaking isn't scalable because you can only be in one place at a time. And you've got a business to run, right? Well, a webinar is just like giving that PowerPoint presentation in front of a room full of people, but with a couple of major differences.

First, webinar campaigns are hugely scalable, able to reach hundreds and even thousands of prospects.

Second, your webinar audience can be anywhere in the world; they don't need to book a flight and a hotel to come see you speak. All they have to do is turn on their computer.

Third, as the speaker, you don't need to spend time and money travelling around the country, either. You can give your presentation wearing pajamas and bunny slippers while sitting on your couch at home. The webinar attendees will only see your computer screen and hear your voice (unless you prefer to turn your webcam on).

And finally, if you record your webinar you can replay it over and over again to new audiences without doing additional work. So you only have to research, write, and create the webinar once. In fact, you could have multiple prerecorded webinars running every week while you're lounging by the pool. Now *that's* scalability!

There are many ways to do webinars. The most common is to simply share your computer screen with your attendees. All they see are your PowerPoint slides and all they hear is your voice. Some webinar presenters choose to also have their computer's webcam enabled, so the audience can see their face. But disabling the webcam makes hosting a webinar much easier, as it leaves you free to look at your notes or even read them straight off the page. For somewhat introverted people like me, this is wonderful.

Pro tip: A webinar is not a teleconference. A teleconference is just a phone call that many people can listen to. There are no visuals and no PowerPoint presentation. Webinars are much more powerful than teleconferences because they engage your audience's eyes as well as their ears. So if you have a choice, I always recommend a webinar rather than a teleconference.

WEBINARS CREATE VALUE

You probably want to do a webinar to sell your product or

generate sales leads. But remember the principles of content sharing! First and foremost you must provide your attendees with real value. They must get something out of the time they're investing in your webinar. You may think lecturing them for an hour about your company's products is value, but trust me, it isn't. If your webinar is a giant product pitch you're just going to irritate your audience. So you have to give them something that they really want: useful, actionable information that will help them in their work.

Instead of pitching product, do some research on your target prospects and find out what they are interested in. What types of problems do they worry about in their business? What are the frequent topics of discussion in your LinkedIn group? What are people complaining about? What topics generate the most comments? Use your research to generate a short list of three to five potential webinar topics.

Next, do a quick survey. Message a few dozen of your prospects or group members and ask them which topic they'd be most interested in learning more about. Webinar success starts with understanding your market and your customers.

For example, you might learn that many companies are looking for creative ways to cut costs at their shareholder meetings or annual conventions. So if you create and plan a webinar titled "Amazing Corporate Events on a Budget" you will likely get many people to sign up. Then when you present the webinar, share plenty of solid, useful information and inside tips for cost cutting. Every attendee will feel it was time well spent because they learned something valuable.

Unlike with a LinkedIn group discussion or message campaign, though, with a webinar you get to include a pitch for your company at the end, and a call to action around a product or service you offer. This works well because once the webinar is finished, you'll have already earned their respect and goodwill for sharing your amazing content, so a short pitch doesn't seem manipulative or underhanded. (Also, since most webinars end with sales pitches these days, most people who sign up for yours will not feel blindsided by you including one.)

One popular tactic for webinars that will work in almost every business is including case studies and success stories. This generally involves telling the story of one company that succeeded in the marketplace and giving a step-by-step analysis of how they did it. People love success stories, and they love learning about what other successful companies are doing.

This works especially well if the product you're selling played a part in their success. For example, if you're a SaaS provider and your software helped the business in the case study succeed, that becomes a natural segue into a sales discussion for your product. "Today I showed you how ABC Inc. used our software to grow by 200%. If you'd like to explore how this solution could generate the same results for you, we'd like to set up a call with one of our account specialists. We'll be reaching out to you in the coming days." Boom!

TYPES OF WEBINARS

Generally there are two broad categories of webinars.

The first type is designed primarily to build brand awareness and generate sales leads. In this type of webinar your goal is to impress the attendees so much with your knowledge and expertise that they agree to a post-webinar meeting or phone call. You already have their contact information at this point, so you simply let them know that "Someone from our organization will be reaching out to you in the next couple days to ask your thoughts on the webinar and discuss some of the ideas we talked about today." This webinar strategy is best for B2B companies, and any company with high-dollar expensive products or services.

The second type of webinar is designed to directly sell something—and the goal is to get attendees to pull out their credit cards and make a purchase immediately. This category of webinar is popular for information products, such as training or coaching programs, as well as many other types of products. If your goal is to make a direct sale at the end of the webinar it is helpful to offer an incentive to buy now.

For example, if you have an information product, like a $99 e-book or a video series that helps personal fitness trainers sign more clients, in your webinar you could share the top ten tips for building a fitness business and wow the audience with your knowledge and expertise. At the end of the webinar, you reveal that there are actually twenty-five tips in total, and all of them are explained in detail in your 100-page e-book...that you can buy right now for 50% off.

Pro tip: There are also webinars that actually charge customers a fee to attend. This strategy works best when the webinar offers very valuable and specialized information that people are willing to pay for upfront. Money-making techniques, career or business advice, and self-help are typical topics in this category. Aside from making a few bucks, another benefit of charging for your webinar is that registrants are much more vested; when they actually have skin in the game, the attendance rate skyrockets. Whereas free webinars typically see attendance rates of 25–40%, paid webinars can see attendance as high as 80%.

That being said, most webinars offer their content for free, and then try to convert attendees at the end.

IS YOUR BUSINESS A GOOD CANDIDATE FOR WEBINARS?

For a webinar strategy to make sense for your business, you generally must have at least a few thousand potential customers. This is because webinars are not a high response rate kind of tactic. After all, you're going to be asking people to dedicate an hour of their time, and many people simply aren't willing to do that, no matter how much they'd like to hear what you have to say. As such, you need a big enough audience to which to market your webinar.

There are also many steps in the webinar sign-up funnel. Potential attendees need to:

- Open the email invitation
- Click the invitation link
- Sign up at the registration page

- Show up at the webinar
- Stay for the whole webinar
- Convert (buy or sign up) at the end

That's a lot of steps, and at each one you will lose people. So in order to have anyone left after all that attrition, you need to start with a decent pool of prospective attendees.

Let me walk through a representative example of some typical numbers. Consider an email list of 10,000 prospects. That's a good-sized universe. You send two rounds of emails marketing your webinar, and the emails average a 15% open rate. So now you're down to 3,000 prospects that even see the promotion. If you then get a 20% click-through on those emails, you're down to 600 prospects that make it to your registration/landing page. If the landing page converts well, maybe 50% of those people will sign up. From those 300, only about 35% will actually attend the webinar. So that's about 105 attendees for your webinar from a total possible pool of 10,000. If you're new to webinars that may not seem like a lot, but it's actually very strong. You should be pleased if you get 100 attendees on your webinars; those are solid numbers.

But now consider a business that only has a total universe of about 500 prospects. Even if they convert well, the same formula would only result in about five attendees. Is it worth all the effort? Maybe. Only you can decide that. If you're selling a product or service that costs $20,000 or $50,000 or $500,000, and those remaining five prospects are hot leads, then yes, it's worth it. It depends on your business and your product. But the key point here is that webinars work best if you have a large universe of potential customers.

For these same reasons, businesses that only operate in a limited geographic area are less likely to have success with webinars. For example, a regional company that only sells products in the city of Cincinnati will have a much smaller universe of potential customers than a company that sells its products all over the country or the world. The smaller your prospect pool, the faster you'll run out of runway.

PLANNING YOUR WEBINAR

Planning a webinar is like planning a fancy party; the longer you wait until the last minute to plan it, the less likely it will be to succeed.

It takes about four weeks to prepare for and promote a quality webinar, if you know what you're doing. Here's why:

- First, it takes time and testing to hone in on the topic that will most appeal to your prospects.
- Second, you have to research, write, create, and produce your webinar content.
- Third, you have to think about what your goal is for your webinar, and plan your strategy and call to action so that at the end of the webinar the attendees will become paying clients.
- And fourth, perhaps most important, you must market and promote your webinar so people will show up. You don't want to do all that work and have only two people in the

audience. I'll cover marketing and promotion in detail in the next chapter.

If you procrastinate too much, you won't be able to do quality work on any of these four tasks. Take content, for example; once you have decided on your topic, it takes time to research information, collect case studies, organize your presentation, build the PowerPoint slides, and practice. Then you should test the presentation in front of your friends or coworkers and ask for their feedback and suggestions. You will probably make small changes and tweaks all the way up until a day or two before the live webinar.

What you *don't* want to do is get behind schedule and have to slap something together that isn't your best work. Remember, your attendees are busy people. They're trusting you to make this webinar worth their time. If you start at least a month out and put in the effort, it will be. I'll show you what steps to take and when in the next chapter.

TIPS AND TRICKS

Here are a few webinar tips and tricks that I've learned over the course of hundreds of webinars. But like many things in life, the best way to learn is by doing, so as soon as you feel you're ready, jump in and try your first webinar. This chapter will give you a good starting point, and you'll keep improving the more experience you get.

- **Make sure you choose webinar topics that people really care about.** This is critical. Choose a topic that adds real value and is worthwhile for your target prospects to attend; otherwise, no one will show up. We'll talk more about how to pick the right topics in the next chapter.

- **Write out your entire talk track word-for-word.** Script it! This may sound like a lot of unnecessary work, but trust me, it's worth it. You've spent a lot of time and effort planning your webinar and getting people to show up, so you want to make darn sure you deliver your message the right way. Don't leave this to chance. There will be a lot of thinking going on in your head during a webinar, so it's easy to forget things, even your key message. Having it all scripted also reduces fear and anxiety. If what you're going to say is written right in front of you, you'll be more relaxed—even if you don't use the script.

- **Write the way you talk.** Don't use fancy words in your script, unless you actually talk that way. Most people use small words, lots of contractions, and sometimes incomplete sentences. Sentence fragments are fine.

- **Practice, practice, practice.** You know the old joke about "How do you get to Carnegie Hall? Practice, practice, practice." Pretend like you'll be giving this webinar in Carnegie Hall. The more you practice, the more confident and relaxed you'll be. It is important to practice so the words seem like you're just talking, not reading, especially if you are going to read word-for-word from a script. The more you rehearse the more natural it will sound. Ask a friend to listen to you over the phone and see if she can tell you're reading a script.

- **Use a professional microphone.** The built-in mic on your computer is fine for Skyping with your friends, but probably inadequate for professional use. Upgrade to an external mic made specifically for webinars. I recommend the Samson Co1U USB studio condenser microphone. You can usually pick one up with a shock mount kit for under $90 from Amazon, sometimes even less on sale.

- **Use GoToWebinar for hosting your live webinars.** There are a number of live webinar solutions out there, and I've tried them all. GoToWebinar is the gold standard. Unfortunately, it's also the most expensive. You can try to save a few bucks with one of the cheapies, but you might end up paying for it later. The cost of one webinar disaster can easily wipe out any small savings from using a lesser solution. Here's a link to get a free trial of GoToWebinar: **LinkedSelling.com/GoToWebinar**

- **Invite someone to co-host the webinar with you.** When two people are presenting a webinar together it often runs a lot more smoothly. Two people can divide up the work, so one person can focus on the slides and presenting while the other person can moderate the chat, organize questions, facilitate, troubleshoot, pop out for coffee, and just chime in once in a while with an observation or a rehearsed ad-lib. Plus, with two hosts, your webinar will seem a little more legit, and make it less likely that attendees will wonder if you're sitting at home wearing a tank-top and board shorts.

- **Prepare questions ahead of time.** At the end of your webinar, when you open it up to questions from the audience, it's awkward if no one asks anything. So I suggest you always have a few questions ready to go. Many webinar hosts even act like those prepared questions came from the audience. Remember, people like to feel as though they're participating in something that's popular and vibrant. If they get the sense that there are only a few people in the webinar, they won't come back.

- **Plant the questions you really want to answer.** Whether you have a full house or a handful of attendees, you always want to make sure you get your business and products promoted at the end of the webinar. An easy way to do this is to "plant" or script a few questions about your product or services to make it seem as though an audience member submitted the question. That way you can talk a bit about your company and products without seeming pushy.

- **Always record your webinars.** This allows you to go back and listen and watch your webinar to self-critique. Make a list of things you could do better next time. Recording also lets you rerun your webinars again and again.

- **Try to keep your webinars evergreen.** In other words, omit any reference to the time of day, day of the week, date, seasons, holidays, the weather, your Christmas tree, jack-o-lanterns, and anything else that would give away the fact that you recorded this webinar six months ago and you're replaying it. This goes for what you say verbally, as well as the text on your slides. If your webinar is evergreen you can record it and run it over and over again.

- **Edit if you have to.** Sometimes you'll want to make a few edits, cut out something stupid you said, or add information. You can use any editing software to do this, like Final Cut Pro or Adobe Premiere. But I find a program called Camtasia simple and easy to use because it's designed as a screen recorder. Here's a link: **LinkedSelling.com/Camtasia**

- **Plan and implement a strong call to action at the end.** A rookie mistake I see a lot is that a good webinar just fizzles out at the end, instead of finishing strong. Do not end your webinar by mumbling to yourself and saying, "Well...uh...I guess that's it...bye." A strong finish needs to be well planned, compelling, definitive, and rehearsed. If your goal is to sell product then and there, have your sales pitch ready to go and say it. Do not end in a wishy-washy puddle of indecisiveness. Practice strong endings.

- **Learn the webinar software ahead of time.** Make sure you know how to work everything and what to click and when. A little practice goes a long way here. You do not want to be using your webinar software for the first time *during* an actual live webinar. I suggest doing a full-on live trial run to test everything.

- **Use automated email software to simplify your email campaigns.** When you are running webinars you need an email system to tell people about your webinar. Send them a link to the landing page, remind them it's coming up, and then follow up after the webinar. GoToWebinar has some built-in email capabilities, but it's far more limited than what you can do with your own email marketing software. My favorite is a full-featured, robust email service called Infusionsoft. Here's a link: **LinkedSelling.com/Infusionsoft.** For a less expensive, more basic option you can also look into MailChimp, which also comes highly recommended. We'll talk much more about email software and how to use it to promote your webinar in the next chapter.

And perhaps most important, *market the heck out of your webinars!* The single most demoralizing mistake people make is not getting enough attendees to show up. This doesn't have to happen! We'll dig in to marketing and promoting webinars to draw maximum attendance in the next chapter.

RECORD AND RERUN YOUR WEBINARS

The super bonus round of scalability in webinar marketing occurs when you create and present your webinar once, record it, then replay that same webinar over and over to a brand new audience every time. That's some serious efficiency. You can do all the hard work one time, and then continue to reap the benefits for years. Luckily there are some really effective tools to easily automate this process.

The platform that I recommend is called StealthSeminar. Here's a link to their site which is filled with tips and information about creating killer webinars: **LinkedSelling.com/StealthSeminar.** StealthSeminar co-founder Geoff Ronning says he created this technology platform because he loves automation, and he wanted to rerun his own webinars to maximize efficiency. Setting up StealthSeminar takes a little effort, but it's not technical, they have amazing support, and you'll get the hang of it in no time.

THE HARDEST PART OF WEBINAR CAMPAIGNS

Creating, practicing, and delivering great webinar content is not the most difficult part of webinar marketing. That's actually the fun part. The hard part is simply getting people to show up—in other words, effectively marketing and promoting the webinar. If you can master this skill you will be a webinar superstar in no time. We'll show you how in the next chapter.

NINE

MARKET, PROMOTE, AND EXECUTE YOUR WEBINAR

Webinars can be a powerful marketing tool for your business... but only if people show up! You can present the most compelling, engaging webinar of the year, but if you only get two people to attend it's an epic fail.

If you're going to put in the work to create and execute your webinar, then you must also put in the effort to market and promote it properly. I would even argue that the marketing requires *more* attention and planning than actually conducting the webinar.

In this chapter we'll run down all the key steps in planning, marketing, and promoting your webinar, and we'll put everything on a timeline so you'll get a sense of when you should be doing what. These are general guidelines, so don't panic if things don't line up 100%. But we've developed them over years of trial and error, so if you follow them you should avoid most of the mistakes I made early on. Just by reading this chapter you'll be light-years ahead of where I started. Let's dive in.

FOUR WEEKS OUT

About a month out, you'll begin your initial webinar preparation. (For your first webinar, you may want to start even earlier, just to give yourself an extra cushion of prep and learning time.) Initial prep will include the following tasks:

1. Pick the webinar date and time. A few things to keep in mind as you make this choice:

Schedule your webinar on a Tuesday, Wednesday or Thursday. Research has shown that these days draw highest webinar attendance. (That said, every audience is different, so it's important that you test to find out what's best for yours.)

If you're selling a B2B product or service, you can schedule the webinar during work hours. 10:00 am or 11:00 am Pacific Time tends to work well, since people in all four US time zones can easily attend at that time.

If you're selling B2C, on the other hand, it's probably a good idea to schedule the webinar outside work hours. Early evening is your go-to time slot here, though over a weekend could also work.

2. Choose your content.

By this point, you'll have already done some research on possible webinar topics that will directly appeal to your prospects. At the four-week mark, start to narrow down the options and decide what information, case studies, and success stories you will present.

Remember, never present a webinar that just focuses on giving a sales pitch for your product or service. No one will sign up for that. If you have a heating and cooling company, do not present a webinar titled, "Features and Benefits of the AirCon5000 Heating and Cooling System." Come up with a title like, "Strategies for Reducing Your Building's Heating and Cooling Costs by 37%." That sounds much more appealing. (And of course, in one of your case studies you can casually mention the AirCon5000.)

3. Choose your webinar title.

I know, we just talked about titles. But we're going to mention them again.

Why?

Because your title is the *most important factor* in marketing your webinar.

Here's a great example. What do you think would happen if we tried to promote a webinar titled "LinkedIn Marketing

Strategies Training Session"? Few people would sign up! Why? Because it's boooorrrinnng.

Don't get me wrong, the content could be solid, but the lame title would scare people away. Your attendees may not judge books by their covers, but they absolutely will judge your webinar by its title. If your title is boring, they'll respond with a resounding "meh"—and not sign up for the webinar.

How to avoid this? Get creative. Choose titles that sound actionable, interesting, and will pique curiosity. Make sure they include tangible benefits for the potential attendees (such as: "The LinkedIn system for generating 1,548 qualified leads in just 18 minutes a day"). It's almost like writing headlines for a magazine; you want to hook people. If your company has a good copywriter on staff, you'll probably want them involved in this process. And don't be afraid to try different titles until you find one that clicks, or even change the title a few weeks out based on the response you've had so far.

4. Create your landing page

One of the most important factors in marketing your webinar is the landing page, also called a registration page. This is the web page where people will be taken once they click on a link to learn more about your webinar. Landing pages are very simple, usually just including a little bit of written copy about the webinar itself and a place to sign up. You can see a good example of a landing page at **LinkedWebinar.com**.

The great thing here is that you can build a landing page and start marketing your webinar before you've even committed to delivering or designing the webinar. That may sound backwards, but I really recommend doing it. Get the landing page up before you spend hours and hours refining your actual presentation. Why? Because depending on how many people actually sign up, the landing page may change completely. And this may force your content to change.

To revisit the example from above, if you create a landing page all about reducing an office building's heating and cooling costs, but no one is signing up, then it's time to change some things. You want to do some research to determine why people aren't signing up. Is it the topic? Is it the wording? Is it the design of the page? Luckily, collecting hard data will answer these questions definitively, and it's pretty easy to do.

Software like LeadPages (**LinkedSelling.com/LeadPages**) is designed to help you create killer landing pages, and then test which ones work best. I like these sites because you don't have to be a techie to make them work (or a Wall Street CEO to afford them). I recommend starting with their preloaded templates and customizing them as needed.

And yes, you read that right: Ideally you should test more than one landing page, and they'll all need to be a little bit different from each other. Why? Because essentially, these programs give you the ability to divvy up incoming web traffic to different landing pages. Then you can look at the conversion rates of each to see which page is converting best (getting the most sign-ups). This is an ongoing process. As you learn which landing pages are working and which are not, you can use that data to help refine your webinar content, title, date and time, etc.

The importance of a good landing page cannot be overstated. It's certainly worth investing the time and effort writing good copy and then testing. A difference of just a few percentage points in conversion rates can have an enormous impact on the number of attendees on your webinar, and your bottom line.

THREE WEEKS OUT:
SET UP YOUR EMAIL AUTO-RESPONDER

Now that your landing pages are set up, it's time to prep the communication system for the people who will sign up. This is your only marketing task this week.

An auto-responder is an automated software program that sends out a sequence of emails to people on a list at predetermined intervals. Why is this important? Because once you have people's names and email addresses on your webinar list, you can reach out to them both before and after the webinar to make sure their webinar experience is amazing. This is an integral part of the webinar's success.

Immediately after they sign up for your webinar, the first email will be a welcome and confirmation email containing the login details and instructions for the webinar. The rest of the emails leading up to the webinar are designed to remind people why they signed up and what they're going to learn, to remind them when the webinar is, and to build anticipation and excitement.

Pro tip: Do *not* schedule a reminder email every day for three weeks. That will just make people angry. Send a couple emails per week, and include some useful content in each email so there's more to it than just a boring reminder. This additional content can include teasers, short case studies, success stories from previous webinars, or even tips and tricks for getting the most out of the webinar. You can also ask for questions that attendees would like to have answered during the webinar.

You don't necessarily need a skilled copywriter to wordsmith each of these emails (though you certainly can use one if you'd like!). Treat them like the content-sharing messages in your messaging campaigns; write in a casual, genuine manner, and try to write the way you talk. Avoid being formal or pushy.

TWO WEEKS OUT

Now it's time to start promoting the webinar! We typically recommend four tactics for promoting your webinar, each targeting a different group of potential attendees.

1. Promote on LinkedIn.

All the work you've done building up your LinkedIn groups and connections will prove tremendously useful for promoting your webinars. Start your promotion efforts there.

First, send out an "announcement" to all of your group members announcing the webinar. Announcements are one of the benefits you have as a group owner. Once a week, you can send a customized message that hits the inbox of all group members.

You should also message your first-degree connections on LinkedIn, inviting them to the webinar. Sending personalized one-to-one messages to your connections, although time intensive, gets a huge response rate. You might be tempted to message your connections in bulk, which is understandable, but it gets nowhere near the results of sending each message one-on-one. People know when they're getting blasted. But when a message is personalized through LinkedIn, it will come across far more genuine and your results will be far greater.

You can also reach out individually to other groups' members, even if you're not connected to them, and tell them about your webinar. You can message anyone on LinkedIn that shares a group with you. And as long as they genuinely look like they'd be a good fit for your webinar, you'll be in good shape! These people have opted to receive messages from other group members when they joined their various groups. (And of course, be sure to include a link to your webinar's landing page in every message so they can click through and sign up.)

Remember to write in a personal and informal way, like you're telling a friend about something special. For example, "Hey, Bobby, it's been great being connected with you here on LinkedIn. I thought you might be interested in a webinar I have coming up. We're going to be talking about X, Y, and Z, and I thought you might be into it. If you'd like to check it out, here's the link. Hope you're doing well." This informal tone will get a much better response rate than sending them a message that's written like a formal marketing brochure.

2. Promote to your in-house email list.

Most businesses have some sort of in-house email list of customers or clients. This is a great list for marketing your webinars. Presumably these people are already familiar with you, your company, and your products, so use your email auto-responder to leverage this list and invite them to join your webinar.

3. Use paid marketing channels to reach entirely new prospects.

Any time you present a webinar, it makes sense to try to bring in some completely new faces. Invite people from outside of your current pool of known LinkedIn contacts and your in-house lists. This is one area where more traditional online marketing techniques can help you. LinkedIn ads, Facebook ads, YouTube ads, Google pay-per-click, Twitter ads, Pinterest ads, and all variety of other online advertising can put your webinar in front of eyes that might never have seen it otherwise. Basically you want to use these tools to reach your prospects wherever they hang out online. You certainly don't need or want to advertise in *all* of the previously mentioned channels; just the ones that give you the best chance of reaching your prospects.

4. Establish joint ventures.

When you partner with someone else who has a large list or following, it's called a joint venture. This is common practice in internet marketing. Once they agree to the joint venture, you'll be able to promote your webinar to their email list as well as yours. How many joint ventures should you do? As many as you can! One joint venture could double, triple, or even quadruple your reach.

Pro tip: Identify other online groups (LinkedIn or otherwise) that have a big list of members that you think would be a good fit for your webinar. Then contact the administrator or owner of that list to see if they'd be willing to promote your webinar to their members. Write something like, "Hey, I noticed you have a community that I think would be a good fit for my webinar. Would you be interested in talking about how we could structure a promotional deal?" More often than not they'll agree as long as there's some benefit for them.

Potential benefits for joint venture partners could include:

- You agree in turn to market their products to your group.
- You compensate them directly.
- You split the sales from your webinar with them, or do a revenue share, or pay them a commission.

If your webinar will add value to their members, they might even let you use the list for free.

We have more training on Linked University on all of these promotional strategies, including scripts and step-by-step instruction on how to put them in place. The best place to start for an introduction to Linked U is by signing up for an upcoming webinar at **LinkedWebinar.com**.

ONE WEEK OUT

The most important task for the week leading up to the webinar is *to make sure everything is working correctly.*

Conduct a "dress rehearsal" of your webinar. Pretend it's really happening live, and run through the entire webinar. If something doesn't go smoothly, or if you forgot an important element, pretend it's live and keep going. It's far better to find any problems a week in advance so you have plenty of time to correct them. Besides, there are almost always minor tweaks to your script and your PowerPoint slides that you'll notice in the dress rehearsal.

1–2 DAYS OUT

The last three emails you will send out through the auto-responder are final reminder emails that come two days before, one day before, and the day of your webinar.

Our research shows that you can still get results promoting your webinar through email and ads up until the time the webinar goes live. Why? Because two weeks or even one week out, a lot of people won't know their schedules for the webinar day yet. So they'll put off signing up, and maybe forget about it entirely. But *one* day out, their schedule is pretty well set; when they get one of those last-minute reminder emails, they might just join the webinar.

Send a separate set of emails out to the people who have already signed up, reminding them of the date and time, and providing login instructions. Typically it's best to send an email the day prior, as well as a final reminder a couple hours before the event. Yes, they've already received this info, but it's always better to send it to them again than to make them dig through their inboxes for it.

20-30 MINUTES OUT: LOG IN, GREET EARLY BIRDS, FINAL TECH CHECK

I usually recommend logging in about twenty to thirty minutes before the start of the webinar. This lets you relax, get your bearings, get comfortable, and make sure everything is working properly. Then, you'll want to start the webinar and begin letting attendees trickle in about ten minutes before the official start time. This provides a good opportunity to greet the early bird attendees and get them talking. Once I see a group of people are logged on, I'll turn on my mic and start greeting them.

I'll say something like, "Hey everyone, Josh Turner here. Thanks for being here this morning. This is going to be awesome. We're definitely going to have a packed house today." I usually have this early greeting scripted. And I always say it's a packed house, no matter what, because again, people like to be a part of something that's vibrant and happening. And attendees can't tell whether there are five people or 500 attending the webinar. (Note: with some webinar systems they can, but not with GoToWebinar.)

Then I usually ask people questions, like where are they from, I ask their name, and make them feel comfortable. People appreciate that sort of personal greeting. It also helps to get the conversation going in the direction of the webinar topic. So I'll ask questions like, "What are the biggest challenges your business is facing today?" The more you get people sharing and talking and interacting, the better the whole thing will go. This chitchat also helps make sure your audio and picture are working; you don't want to be ten minutes into the webinar only to find out people can't hear you.

One important note: If at all possible, do not conduct your webinar on a computer connected to the Internet via a Wi-Fi signal. If you have a choice between a laptop using Wi-Fi and a desktop that is hard-wired to the Internet, choose the hard-wired computer. As reliable as Wi-Fi is, it's still a risk. If your connection is shaky and the audio or picture is popping in and out, people will drop out of the webinar.

CONDUCT YOUR WEBINAR

At this point you have a full house of attendees, you've warmed them up, you're well prepared, you're calm, and you're ready to begin. When delivering your webinar, just relax and be yourself—but be the version of yourself when you're excited and enthusiastic about something. Even if you're introverted and quiet, you can still be excited and enthusiastic. If the audience senses you're bored and just trying to get through it, they'll tune out. So get pumped up! Show your passion for what you're presenting. Make sure the attendees think you're excited to be there. One trick to help with this is to vary the speed of your delivery. Speed up, slow down, and even whisper at times. Change your vocal intonation to emphasize key points. This will take some practice, but it'll become second nature before you know it.

Pro tip: After a while, you will develop your own delivery style. One of the best ways to learn about different styles is to sign up for and attend other webinars, preferably those conducted by experienced, well-known marketers. There are plenty of them out there on all manner of different topics. So even if you are not particularly interested in the content, it's a good idea to attend as many webinars as you can. It's valuable research. And of course, you'll learn a ton by continuing to do your own webinars. You'll get better each time.

FOLLOW UP AFTER YOUR WEBINAR

Your email auto-responder will also come into play after the webinar is over. Shortly after the webinar ends, an email should be sent to all the attendees thanking them for their time, and asking for their feedback or to take a short survey about the webinar. Depending on your goals, you can also use this email to make a product offer or request a sales call. Plan out ahead of time your strategy to get these webinar attendees into your sales pipeline. We'll show you some specific strategies for doing this in the next chapter.

LET US DO IT FOR YOU

If you're getting the sense that marketing and promoting webinars takes a lot of work and involves managing a lot of moving parts, you're right. There's really no secret sauce and no hidden shortcuts to organizing and managing a killer webinar campaign. I wish there were. You just have to put in the work and do the heavy lifting. But it's well worth it, especially once your webinars are set up on a system like Stealth Seminar and running on autopilot.

If you put enough time and effort into it, I know you can succeed at becoming a webinar superstar and making webinars an effective part of your marketing mix.

But not every company has the bandwidth and available manpower to orchestrate a webinar campaign. Not to worry!

We have a division of our company called Webinarli. We've assembled an experienced team of webinar professionals who do nothing but run professional webinar campaigns for clients. They'll plan, market, promote, and run your entire webinar strategy, so you can focus on your core business. We've worked out all the bugs to create a portfolio of best practices that virtually guarantees you'll become a webinar superstar in the shortest possible time. Visit **Webinarli.com** to check out more details and sign up for a consultation.

If you like the idea of using webinars to generate leads and sales, but you don't think you're ready to manage a campaign on your own, let us do it for you.

Mertz-International

Mertz-International LLC is a consulting firm specializing in tax planning for U.S. expatriates in Asia and Russia. Firm owner and managing partner Mike Mertz knew that growing only through referrals was limiting his business. But where else could he find prospects? After all, "U.S. expatriates in Asia" isn't a search filter offered anywhere we know of. Utilizing some creative processes within LinkedIn, we were able to find a virtually limitless supply of these prospects to target for Mertz-International's campaign. And our process for reaching them has generated a substantial increase in revenue for the firm.

DESIGNING THE CAMPAIGN

To begin, we used a number of unconventional advanced searches and criteria to find a large pool of prospects to target on LinkedIn. From there, we worked with Mertz-International to design a campaign that would directly connect with these prospects, work them through a short-term nurture campaign, and culminate fairly quickly with a direct call to action. After deciding that the best prospect profile to utilize would be the owner himself, Mike Mertz, we were ready to get started. The campaign required a short setup phase, where our team directly connected Mike with hundreds of prospects using his LinkedIn account.

Also during the setup phase, we got Mike into the right Linkedln groups where his prospects were actively engaged. We optimized his profile to help convert views into leads. And we began building the content and messaging that would be utilized for the top-of-mind nurture component of the campaign.

LAUNCHING THE CAMPAIGN

Once we completed the setup phase, we were ready to roll out the ongoing monthly campaign. We maintained top-of-mind awareness with all of Mike's connections, as well as thousands of additional prospects that exist in his LinkedIn groups, through daily status updates and bi-weekly group postings.

Posting these updates alone, however, didn't generate a flood of leads. Sure, an inbound lead came in every once in a while, but with the consistent outreach and behind-the-scenes messaging generating leads like clockwork, Mike no longer needed to wait around for word-of-mouth hot leads to walk into his office.

RESULTS

As a direct result of prospects targeted via the LinkedIn campaign, Mike's firm has generated twenty-nine new paying clients in the last eight months. The campaign is ongoing, so we'll undoubtedly see this number rise even more. Mike sees a steady stream of new qualified leads rolling into his LinkedIn inbox every month. And with the messaging campaign warming up these prospects prior to the call, nearly 50% of his leads from LinkedIn have converted into paying customers!

From an ROI standpoint, Mike's investment in the campaign is generating roughly two times his firm's investment in first-year revenue alone. Considering the lifetime value of a client, the long-term ROI is tremendous.

If the tactics in this book worked for Mertz-International, they will work for your company too. Thanks for reading, and good luck!

TEN

FOLLOW UP AND CONVERT YOUR WEBINAR LEADS

I briefly explained in Chapter 9 that you should plan and script the end of your webinar, and that you should have a clear goal for what you want to accomplish. One goal might be to sell a product right on the webinar. Other goals could be to build brand awareness, to move prospects deeper into your sales funnel, or to schedule a follow-up sales call. This chapter will teach you how to accomplish that goal.

The key is to think about your end goal from the very beginning, so it can inform and influence your decisions as you plan your webinar content and strategy. Choose case studies and content that set up your sales pitch for your product or service. During the planning stages, look for tie-ins and connections between your audience, your content, your goals, and your product.

For example, if you're presenting a webinar to commercial construction executives, and your product is concrete, and your goal is to schedule a sales call, look for content and case studies that bridge the gap between this audience, product, and goal.

Of course it's crucial that all the content is very good, but because you're using these webinars as a sales tool, the way you end your webinar is equally critical. Always close your webinar in a way that gets people pulling out their credit card to purchase your product or service, filling out a survey form, or requesting a phone call for a consultation or strategy session—whatever the next step is. In this chapter we'll explore some of the most effective post-webinar strategies for follow-up and conversion.

PRIORITIZE YOUR PROSPECTS

If you only have thirty prospects show up for your webinar, you can easily reach out to every one of them with a personalized sales call after it's over. And you should. But let's say you hit a home run with your webinar and 2,000 people signed up. Wow! That means your topic was a hit, and your prospects were eager to hear what you had to say. Congrats! Now comes the hard part. You can't call all 2,000 webinar attendees on the phone—at least not in the week or two after the webinar (unless you have a pretty big sales team). So you have to prioritize those 2,000 attendees.

In every webinar, there are generally three different tiers of prospects:

- Tier 1: hot prospects who are ready to buy right away
- Tier 2: warm prospects who are interested in learning more
- Tier 3: prospects who are not ready to buy right now, but might be at some point in the future (most of your attendees will fall into this category)

You can often tell which ones are the hot Tier 1 leads because they are highly engaged in the webinar conversation, they post a lot of comments in the chat, and ask lots of questions. They may even directly request a call with you. These are the top-tier prospects you want to go after first. Follow up with them right away.

After you work the hottest prospects through your sales process, then gradually move on to the Tier 2 warm leads. These are the webinar attendees who were somewhat engaged, but not as much as the top-tier prospects. Finally you can start reaching out to the Tier 3 cool leads. Since they didn't express a lot of interest, and maybe didn't even attend, the way you reach out to them will be different than with the first two tiers.

WARM UP THE COOL LEADS

Cool leads are people who registered for the webinar but didn't attend. For this group of prospects it's usually best to warm them up a bit with an email campaign starting immediately after the webinar. Even if you have their phone number, email is the way to approach these people. Calling them when they didn't express much interest on the webinar will come off as super sales-y.

Instead, you can use your email auto-responder to send them a series of emails inviting them to watch a replay of the webinar recording, sharing some fresh content, and then culminating with a request for a phone call.

HEAT UP THE WARMER LEADS

For those prospects who did attend the webinar, there is also still work to be done. Use your email auto-responder to continue to warm them up as you make time to call them.

Here's what the emails you send them could look like:

- The first email is designed to thank the attendees, and to invite them to contact you directly with any additional questions.
- Then a series of emails over the next couple weeks can include reminders of a few key concepts from the webinar, new tips and tricks, related information on the topic, and links to some suggested resources.
- Finally, send a request for a phone call or an opportunity to take a next step together.

This campaign is different from a long-term nurture campaign; it's designed to warm up the attendees enough to request a phone call very shortly after the webinar—within a couple of weeks at most.

If someone is not opening your post-webinar emails, consider them a cold prospect. But if they open all of your emails after the webinar and click on the links, they are a warm lead. Your email marketing software should be able to give you this data. This process can help you further zero in on your list of target prospects.

TAKE IT INTO THE REAL WORLD

The Internet, digital platforms like LinkedIn, and webinars can be powerful sales tools, no doubt about it. And the results can be amazing. But don't fall into the trap of thinking that the day after your webinar hundreds of prestigious clients are going to be filling your inbox with purchase orders; you're still going to have to put on your salesperson hat and close those sales.

If you are selling a product of modest price and asking people to buy it during the webinar, you will probably never have to take the sales process into the real world. You can do it all digitally. But for higher-priced products and services, at some point you will have to leave the digital part of the sales funnel and meet your prospects in the real world. In other words, make a real sales call. It could be over the phone or via GoToMeeting or Skype, and if it's a big enough potential client, you may be getting on a plane and travelling for an actual face-to-face meeting.

All of the automation, digital platforms and strategies in this book are designed to *get you to that real world sales call.* So let's talk about a few strategies for setting up those important sales calls and meetings.

A SIMPLE SLIDE

The most basic technique to ask for a sales call happens during your webinar. Put up a simple PowerPoint slide at the end of your webinar with your contact information on it, and ask people to get in touch. A standard talk track goes something like, "If you're interested in talking more about how this could work for your business, here is my email and phone number. Please contact me and we can set up a complimentary consultation."

There are pros and cons to this approach. On the plus side, this can be a pretty effective method of getting your most enthusiastic prospects to take that next step. It's also simple and easy to execute. There are no online forms to build out, and no web development is required.

Unfortunately, this tactic puts you in the position of waiting for prospects to call you. So you have less control over the sales process. Prospects that are tepid or on the fence may never get around to calling you. Unless they really need your product or service right away, they'll probably want to take their time and think about it, and once it's not right in front of them anymore, they may let it slide entirely.

So depending on your business, a simple slide may be all you need. It's straightforward, easy, and it can be very effective. But in general, relying *solely* on a slide like this is often too passive to get the results you want. Let's look at a few more proactive tactics.

THE FEEDBACK PHONE CALL

Many companies—from Verizon and AT&T to the cable TV company—routinely perform survey calls. People are accustomed to these types of phone calls. So after your webinar you won't surprise too many people by calling to ask for feedback. But you'll use a very specific tactic within your feedback calls. Here's how that works:

- First, you call an attendee and say something like, "I am calling to ask for your feedback on the webinar you attended last week. What did you like or not like about it?" This will get them talking about the webinar.
- Once they've shared their feedback, you ask, "Have you been able to take concrete steps to implement some of the strategies that were discussed in the webinar?" Most people will respond that they have not had a chance because they're too busy, or they have other more pressing matters. That is the opening for you to segue into a sales call.

In response, you could say something like, "If finding the time is a challenge for you right now, have you thought about letting our company implement and manage the process for you? We can take that whole project off your plate and get you similar results, without your having to spend time on it." Just like that, you've started a sales conversation with them about how your services work and what benefits you can provide.

THE SCARCITY CLOSE

Another effective way to get prospects to take action after your webinar is based on a kind of scarcity model. With this tactic, you inform the webinar attendees that you can *only* take on six or eight new clients at this time (or one or two, the exact number is up to you), so they will have to fill out an application to work with you.

The talk track goes like this: "If you'd like to achieve the type of success we showed you in the case studies today, we have a proven program that works. But we only work with clients who are the exact right fit for our services, and we only have room for six new clients at this time. So here is a link to an application page. Fill it out and we'll contact you one way or the other. We can usually let you know within a couple days if it seems like it's going to be a good fit."

This type of close builds excitement and exclusivity into your service. It also allows you to ask for detailed information on the application form, so you can follow up with these prospects later, armed with more information about them and their business.

LONG-TERM CAMPAIGNS

Keep in mind that, like all sales processes, converting webinar attendees into customers is a numbers game. No matter how good you are, you will never convert 70–80% of your prospects. On a really good day a skilled marketer can convert maybe 20–30%. No matter how awesome your product is, most people are not going to be interested in buying or engaging with your company *right now*. They may be interested, but it just isn't the right time for that kind of investment, or they've got too many fires to put out already, or they just aren't ready yet.

So with the majority of your webinar attendees you will have to make a long-term commitment to stay in front of them and earn their trust over time. The webinar thus becomes the beginning of the relationship. It allows you to make a positive first impression, even though that person is not in the market for your product or service right now. So these prospects should be moved into your long-term email "nurture" campaign.

Much like with your LinkedIn messaging campaigns, you can send regular emails to these long-term nurture prospects sharing pertinent content, and even inviting them to future webinars. Eventually they will become familiar and comfortable with you, so when they're ready to buy they will think of you.

LEARN BY DOING

Anyone can start learning how to achieve webinar success by reading books like this one and attending other webinars, but at some point you just need to learn by doing. You've got to bite the bullet and put on your first webinar.

When I hosted my first webinar, I had no idea what to do. I was nervous. And I didn't know if it would succeed or be an epic flop. But I thought to myself, "If these other people can do it, and they're having success with it, then I can surely figure it out too." And I was right. We have figured it out and our business has grown dramatically as a result of webinars. For example, in 2010 I did only a handful of webinars; this year, we will probably do between 700 and 1,000. That's two or three webinars *per day*. And we expect to attract roughly 120,000 people to these webinars!

Many of those are live webinars, but most will be automated reruns of recorded webinars. And because most of the system now runs on autopilot, we can spend our time focusing on marketing the webinars and working prospects through our sales process after the webinars. The process just keeps expanding and generating more leads.

My point here is that before I could build up to that point, I had to do my first webinar. So now it's time for you to just go out and do yours. Follow the steps in these pages, pick a date, research your topic, choose a title, set up your landing page, and start marketing your webinar. Once you have your first webinar under your belt, you'll be much more confident and you will have learned a lot. The second webinar will be easier and better, and the third even easier and even better. Like many things in life, they key is just to start moving forward and do it.

ELEVEN

LATHER, RINSE, REPEAT

Let's dive a little deeper into the real power of webinars, which I refer to as the "Lather, rinse, repeat" technique. As we discussed in Chapter 8, when you record all of your webinars you can set up an automated system to replay them to new audiences over and over again. This allows you to do all the hard work of creating a webinar just *once*. Then you can leverage that hard work many times in the future to reach a much bigger total audience. This is how webinars are incredibly scalable.

The power of taking all of that effort and plugging it into an automated system that runs continuously on autopilot is awesome. It allows you to scale up from doing just a handful of webinars each year to literally hundreds, generating thousands of new leads. Here are a few specific strategies to make "Lather, rinse, repeat" work for you.

ENCORE! ENCORE!

Sometimes a television network will employ an encore strategy to get the most possible viewers for a new TV series. Here's how it works: The TV series premiere may be on a Tuesday night. Then the network will announce an "encore presentation" that same week just a few days later, often on a Friday night. Because completely different people watch TV on those two different nights, the network gets more viewers to sample their new show. You can do the same thing with webinars; simply rerun them just a day or two later to a different audience.

An encore presentation is a quick and easy way to leverage all the hard work you do on each webinar so that more people will see it. Let's say you create, promote, and present your original live webinar on a Wednesday at 11:00 am. But you notice that less than half of the people who signed up actually showed up.

So shortly after the webinar is over, you send out a new email announcing an "encore presentation" the following day at 6:00 pm. Then at 6:00 pm the next day, you rerun a recording of the webinar. We always set up the encore on a different day and at a much different time, because that new time might work better for some people, or for people in different time zones.

The email might say something like, "Yesterday's webinar was a tremendous success. We received rave reviews. But we also heard from many of you who either couldn't make it yesterday or had to hop off early. So we're doing it again! If for some reason you couldn't attend yesterday's webinar, or if you just want to review the things that we talked about, then I'd love to have you join us Thursday evening."

This strategy has several benefits:

- First, you can get more people to see your webinar. By running an encore you can nearly double your total audience.
- Second, even though you get twice the audience, you only have to do the live presentation once. So you get twice the benefit with just a little bit more work.
- Third, you may even get some people who attend both presentations. You know these people are very interested and are likely to be hot prospects.
- And fourth, you can use some of the automation tools we talked about earlier in the book to set up this process on an ongoing basis.

AUTOMATE THE PROCESSES

Remember StealthSeminar from Chapter 8? They're the people who set you up to replay your previously recorded webinars. These people help build your landing pages and completely automate your recorded webinars to run over and over. And every time it will appear to the audience like a brand new, live webinar. It works so well it's scary. Visit LinkedSelling.com/StealthSeminar to get started.

Pro tip: Most companies let these previously recorded webinars appear as if they're live. This tends to create more excitement, drives audience engagement, and boosts authenticity, which gets more people to sign up. Marketing a webinar as "previously recorded" always leads to lower turnout, since it doesn't appear as a special event anymore. So while I would never recommend saying that a previously recorded webinar is live (never lie to your prospects!), it's generally considered okay to just not mention it at all. Most audience members will assume it's live, and what they don't know won't hurt them.

DON'T PESTER PEOPLE

There is a limit to how often you can promote your webinars to the same potential audience. If you keep telling someone week after week about the same webinar, they're going to see you as a pest, and probably unsubscribe from your list altogether.

The same goes for your LinkedIn groups. If you keep telling your group members about the same webinar every week, they're going to tune you out. Or worse yet, they'll leave your group. So you really only want to promote any given webinar to the same audience once every couple of months or so.

MANAGE YOUR LISTS

As you start to create more and more live webinars, run encores, and rerun previously recorded webinars, it's critically important that you manage your email lists efficiently. With programs like Infusionsoft and MailChimp, you can easily select which lists receive which email marketing sequences. With these programs, when people sign up for a particular webinar they're automatically tagged in the system as having signed up for that specific webinar. Infusionsoft calls this a campaign.

By signing up for a particular campaign, that person will now receive the emails in that campaign until they exit it. You can also include and exclude certain lists from receiving emails based on tags that you set up. It's important to actively manage your lists to avoid making mistakes or duplications. You don't want someone who already signed up for or attended a certain webinar to keep getting invitations or marketing emails for the same webinar!

As you rerun your previously recorded webinars, you will need to find new audiences. This is where traditional online marketing comes into play. You can use Facebook ads, LinkedIn ads, joint ventures, and all of the tactics we discussed in previous chapters. With all of these channels you simply continue running your webinar ads until your click-through rates start to decline, and conversion costs begin to rise. When the decline starts, simply change marketing channels, rewrite your ad copy, and keep trying.

CREATE YOUR OWN WEBINAR LIBRARY

After a year or two, you may find that you have created a whole library of webinars on multiple topics tailored to different audiences. Some companies have chosen to create a section on their website dedicated to past webinars. That way people can visit the webinars page and click on the various topics to watch whatever webinar interests them. You can ask people to sign up with an email address before gaining access to the webinar library, and then use this data to market new live webinars to them.

YOU DON'T NEED TO BE A TECHIE

One final thought on automating your webinar process: It sounds more difficult than it really is. In reality there's not much technical about it. The vendors I recommend are easy to work with, and their products are simple and straightforward. If you can work Facebook and LinkedIn, you can run webinar campaigns.

It'll take some time to set it up and work out the kinks. Marketing all these webinars on an ongoing basis can be intensive. But if you take it at your own pace, and slowly expand and ramp up as you get more experience, you'll do just fine.

Before you know it you'll be a webinar guru, raking in sales leads and creating new webinars with great success.

TWELVE

CLOSING THE SALE

What to Do Once You're on the Phone

There's one part of the sales process we haven't talked much about yet. We've worked your prospects all the way through various systems to your call to action: requesting a phone call. But what do you do once you get on the phone with them? I'd be really lame to tell you everything else and leave you hanging once you picked up the phone! So in this chapter we're going to tackle how to close the sale once you've got your awesome prospect on the phone with you.

As you work this system, there are six types of sales calls or conversations that you might find yourself in. Yes, I said six. Why so many different kinds of calls? Because there are different types of prospects and different types of lead gen approaches. Thus, once you're face to face or on the phone, the conversation will be a bit different for each of them. These six cover the majority of situations you'll encounter.

Here are the six types of calls, from the coldest to the hottest.

1. The Cold Call

2. The Warm Cold Call

3. The Networking Call

4. The Carrot Call

5. The Hot Lead Call

6. The Webinar Call

In this chapter we'll take a look at each of them and dig into what they are, how they fit into the system and how you should approach each of them. But first, here's a quick tip that applies to almost all of them.

Pro tip: Slow down!

Whether you're a seasoned sales pro or a business owner doing it all yourself, it's tempting to start your sales call with the product or service you want to sell. Don't do it! The worst thing you can do is jump on a call with a prospect and immediately start telling them all about what you do.

In every type of call, except for the Cold Call, you'll want to start by asking an icebreaker question. Something as simple as where they live usually gets the job done. "So Bob, remind me again what part of the country you're in?" Immediately you'll be engaged in a conversation about Bob's personal life, which is the best way to break through and really get people talking.

(Of course, if you're operating on a more local level, the question will be slightly different. "So Bob, what part of town is your office in? Oh, awesome. Do you live around there too?" You get the point.)

Be prepared to engage the prospect in a conversation here. Don't just say, "Oh, San Francisco, I heard that's a nice place. Well, thanks for taking this call today. What my company does is..." No, no, no. They'll see through that right away. Take the time to genuinely engage with them!

Depending on how engaging the conversation feels, and how interested the prospect seems in the conversation, this small talk can often go on for one to five minutes, sometimes even more! Don't be afraid to really get personal and let it go as far as the prospect will let you take it. Remember, people work with people they know, like and trust. And there's no better way to achieve that kind of status than to get personal!

Even if you can't become best friends in the first few minutes, making small talk is still essential. If you don't feel like you're good at small talk, calls like these are great opportunities to practice.

Now let's jump into each of the types of calls you or your sales team will be making, and how to handle them.

THE COLD CALL

If you implement the system as outlined in this book, you won't be making many of these calls. But if you have a larger sales team or simply do well with cold calling, then this might be a fit for you.

To utilize LinkedIn to boost your cold calling efforts, it's as simple as using the advanced people search to find prospects the way we described back in Chapter 4. From there, you can use software like eGrabber's Account Researcher tool (get a free trial at **LinkedSelling.com/AccountResearcher**) to find phone numbers, or use any other number of tools that do the same thing. And voila, you've got a quality list to start calling!

I'm not going to get into cold calling scripts and best practices here—it's not something I teach and I think the techniques outlined in this book are much more effective. But what I will say is that LinkedIn can seriously supercharge a cold calling campaign. With a prospect's LinkedIn profile in front of you, you're armed with all sorts of data that a traditional "list" can't offer: where they went to school, people they're friends with, other places they've worked, things they're interested in, you name it. Super powerful.

Again though, most people reading this book will never make a completely cold call. So let's jump ahead. The other five types of calls will definitely apply to you.

THE WARM COLD CALL

29% of prospects that you work through this nurture system

will agree to a meeting. But what about the remaining 71%? Should we just forget about them?

Heck no! Those people have been exposed to a ton of content over the course of the campaign. Many are in your LinkedIn group and receive daily or weekly updates. They're all connected to you and see your status updates. And they all just got done receiving a series of personal messages from you over the course of two to three months. You've put forth a lot of effort to get them to this point; don't give up on them so easily.

Now, you might be thinking, "But what can I do at this point, if they haven't agreed to a meeting or call?"

Just pick up the phone and call them!

Here's how that conversation might go. "Hey Danny, this is Josh Turner. You and I are connected on LinkedIn and I shot you a message or two last week about jumping on a call?" That question mark is not a typo. Pose the statement as a question, which infers to them that you're looking for acknowledgement. Most of them will respond with something like, "Yeah, that's right, I did get your messages. Sorry, I meant to get back to you, but I've been really busy." Boom!

Now you're in. More or less, they just acknowledged that they're open to talking. And now you got 'em on the phone. So the next thing you say is, "No worries, I know how it is. How does right now work for you? Do you have a couple minutes?"

If they say no, then try to schedule another time then and

there. Many will say yes though. At that point, move to the script for the Networking Call.

THE NETWORKING CALL

Let's step back for a second and look at the messaging script that most likely got the prospect to agree to this call. It probably goes something like this:

Danny,

I'm trying to get to know my connections on LinkedIn a little better so that we both might benefit from being connected. We've been crossing paths on LinkedIn for the past couple of months and I'd love to schedule a quick call.

Would you have a few minutes to chat next week? How does your calendar look next Wednesday morning?

Thanks,

Josh

You can see how this is positioned as more of a networking call; the prospect isn't necessarily telling you that they want what you're selling. They're agreeing to chat, to learn more about each other's businesses.

Here's how to handle those conversations.

Step 1: Ask them about their business. Think about what

things you have in common, and bring up small talk around those issues. You can talk about the industry, people you both know, things like that. "Tell me more about what you're up to these days?" is a great opening question.

Step 2: Once they start telling you about their business, keep asking follow-up questions. Be genuinely interested in what they're telling you! Spend the first ten minutes talking exclusively about them and their business.

Step 3: During this conversation, listen for pain points and needs they have. Ask questions strategically to get to these issues. The more questions you ask, the more people will open up!

Step 4: Come back to them and say, "Honestly Danny, I wasn't sure where this conversation would go. But I figured since we've been crossing paths there might be some benefit to learning more about what each other is up to. What I heard you say earlier about X, Y, Z...it really made me think that you might be interested to hear about what my company does. Because we've worked with a lot of companies similar to yours, like A, B, and C [name drop some companies similar to theirs], and solved X, Y and Z by doing D, E and F [your solution]. Does that sound like something you'd be interested in hearing more about?"

Step 5: The prospect will say, "Yeah, sure," 99% of the time. If it's framed the right way, a smart businessperson will feel stupid by not agreeing to at least hear you out.

Step 6: Talk to them about your solution and get them to a next step. That could be a second conversation, an in-person meeting, or maybe a proposal. Whatever it is, the goal of the initial call is to move the prospect toward this next step.

Simple as that!

Naturally, not every prospect will move from a Networking Call to becoming a client. But that's sales; it's a numbers game. Some percentage will move deeper in your funnel. The rest can be moved into a more long-term nurture bucket.

THE CARROT CALL

So unless you're pitching Bugs Bunny, this type of call won't involve actual carrots. The carrot we're talking about is a metaphorical carrot, the kind you dangle in front of someone to entice them to get on a call with you!

Here's what that approach might look like:

Hey Danny,

We've been crossing paths here on LinkedIn for a bit and I thought it wouldn't hurt to reach out.

My company has worked with Company X, Y and Z [companies that your prospect would know] to help them [insert result] by [measurable increase/decrease].

I thought you might be interested to hear about how we did it.

If you'd be open to a call, let me know!

Josh

The exact script will vary significantly since each prospect's business is different. The key, though, is to offer some intrigue. Get them thinking, "Holy cow, I gotta learn more about that."

Then, when you get them to agree to the call, you can spend pretty much the entire time sharing case studies with them about how that technique helped various clients. It's your technique and your clients, of course, but relating those things like case studies is super engaging for your prospect. And if your offering is impressive, by the end they'll be eager to learn more about working with you.

There's an important disclaimer here, though; this tactic typically only works for companies that are doing something fairly unique in the market, or have a strong differentiator.

If you're company is really just a "me too" player in a commoditized space, the networking approach will work far better.

Dangling a carrot doesn't work so well when the prospect has a pile of carrots sitting at their feet.

THE HOT LEAD CALL

From time to time, you'll have a prospect on LinkedIn reach directly out to you and express interest in your services. Often times these will be prospects that are in your LinkedIn group, are already connected to you, or just found your awesome, optimized LinkedIn profile. Without even knowing it, the system has warmed them up for you...and served 'em up red hot!

These are those hot leads that you always want. You can't just sit back and rely on them, as most of your calls won't be hot lead calls. But when they show up, they are always a great bonus for your business.

Handling these types of calls is pretty straightforward.

The prospect is already interested in learning more about what you do. Thus, the agenda for the call is simply to a) build rapport and get them engaged in some small talk, then b) chat with them about your services, answer any questions they have, and get them to commit to a next step. It doesn't get much better than that!

THE WEBINAR CALL

Generally speaking, there are two types of webinar calls. One is for the prospects who are immediately interested after your webinar. These people can be handled pretty much the same as a hot inbound lead. They know all about you, and are ready to talk turkey. Use the Hot Lead Call outline for these people.

The second type of webinar call is more akin to a hybrid between the Warm Cold Call and a Hot Lead. Because they've seen your webinar, it's easy to give them a call and say something like, "Hey Danny, I noticed that you signed up for our webinar last week and just wanted to get your feedback on it. Do you have a couple minutes? Great! So what'd you think about it?"

At this point, they'll share their thoughts and most likely will open up about whether or not they feel your solutions are a good fit for them. Almost immediately you'll be knee-deep in a sales conversation.

Make sure to pull back and learn more about their business too, though. It's tempting in this kind of conversation to focus just on your services, but you still need to build rapport. Remember to spend way more time asking them questions than you do telling them about your solution. Following that golden rule will generate dividends, even if you take away nothing else from this chapter.

For more training on improving your sales process, here are a few of the go-to resources that I recommend to my clients:

- Lisa Sasevich – You can get a copy of her free book "Boost Your Sales!" at: LinkedSelling.com/LisaSasevichFreeBook
- Dov Gordon – Dov's manual "How to Systematically and Consistently Attract First-Rate Customers" is pure gold. Normally $97, I've secured a deal to get you a copy of the manual for free at this link: LinkedSelling.com/DovGordon
- Bill Baren – If coaching or consulting is your business, you need to sign up for one of Bill Baren's next webinars. Sign up for the next one here: LinkedSelling.com/BillBaren
- Some more people I follow and highly recommend include: Jack Daly, Jeffrey Gitomer, and Gulliver Giles. If you need

to improve your sales process, any of these people or resources will be a great asset for you.

Improving the effectiveness of your sales process will have a huge impact on the results you are able to get from my system. Naturally, if you can't close, then all the leads in the world will do you no good. Be sure to check out the above resources if you need help in any of those areas!

QUICK WINS

When and How to Use Cold Messaging Strategies

Everything you have seen up to this point puts extreme importance on nurturing relationships before you go in for the sale, and taking time to develop cold prospects so that they know, like and trust you.

Does that mean that you should just dismiss cold messaging?

Not necessarily.

Cold messaging is definitely alive and well. When done properly, it might actually be the cornerstone of your marketing. So don't rule it out just yet!

Cold messaging can be viewed as a similar approach to cold calling, almost like cold calling 2.0. For years cold calling was a pillar for sales teams, but it's lost a lot of its impact in recent years. Sure, many sales teams still do lots of cold calling, but many do it because they have no idea what else to do. Even though it remains largely ineffective for them, they keep at it because it's what they've always done.

Because of cold calling's decline, many people now believe that cold messaging is also a worthless endeavor. After all, at face value there doesn't seem to be any real differences between cold messaging and cold calling.

But upon closer examination, cold messaging can actually yield much stronger results than cold calling. Why? Simply because phone lines are much more closely guarded than LinkedIn inboxes. Spend some time trying to get through on the phone to a cold prospect and you'll likely be stopped at the gates by an assistant—who may not even deliver your message to your prospect. But a LinkedIn cold message is much easier to get through to the target. There's rarely a guardian assistant standing over their LinkedIn account.

Also, there are ways to optimize the methods used to deliver cold messages, enabling you to send a much higher volume of messages than cold calls for a given period of time. Since this is a numbers game, the more messages you deliver, the greater the results. Even though getting on the phone is arguably much more powerful than sending an email, messaging makes up for this by being massively scalable. You simply can't hit the numbers with cold calling that you can with cold messaging.

Given that scalability, cold messaging is extremely powerful in the right situations. Knowing how and when to utilize the cold message tactic, along with knowing what type of message to deliver, will create some pretty amazing results.

That said, it is still a relatively low response activity. Just like cold calling, cold messaging will only generate a small response rate. Typically 5% is what we aim for, which is obviously much lower than the 29% average we expect from a long-term nurture campaign.

As such, this strategy is best suited when you have a massive prospect pool and can afford to get a lower response rate, or if what you sell just isn't amenable to the nurture approach.

One final note: This tactic is definitely not for everybody. You need to have the right situation to make this type of playbook work for you and your business, but if it is indeed the right playbook to run, the results can be awesome. Let's take a look at how to get those kinds of results.

WHEN TO UTILIZE COLD MESSAGING

Cold messaging is a fantastic way to pitch smaller-priced products and services, or to get people to opt-in for something like a webinar or white paper.

Let's say that you are a tax consultant that specializes in providing services to a couple of specific industries and that your clients generally engage with you for $500 or even $1,000 per deal. Cold messaging is going to be a great tactic for you.

Why? Because there are not as many factors that go into a signing a $1,000 deal as there are that go into a five, six, or seven-figure deal. The risk is much lower. You don't need to build up as much trust first. There are fewer people to consult with—often the decision makers you pitch will be able to decide to make the purchase themselves, rather than asking their boss's boss's boss.

On the other hand, if you're a software company that typically sells products or services starting at $50,000 per engagement, then chances are slim that someone will engage with you just from a cold message pitching your product or service.

Sometimes your cold message won't even ask for any sort of sale. You could simply be focused on getting prospects to opt-in for a white paper, case study, or webinar. Then it becomes an even simpler decision for the prospect. They don't need to think about the cost of taking the next step, because there isn't any cost.

This opt-in method can be a much better way to utilize cold messaging to engage with targets you want to sell high-priced products or services. If your cold message was about an $80,000 deal, many targets won't give you the time of day because they don't know you and that's a huge amount of cash to lay out to someone they don't know. But if you ask the same target to opt-in for your webinar, they'll perceive no risk at all, allowing you to build some trust before you actually pitch them.

What about sending a cold message requesting to talk on the

phone? There's no risk or cost to talking on the phone, so it should be easy to get people to accept that, right?

Well, not exactly.

There are a couple of problems with this line of thought. High-priced services and products are almost always pitched to high-level execs. What sounds like merely asking for a call to you comes off to them that you are asking for some of their most valuable resource: their time. A CEO or CFO's time is extremely valuable and limited. Half an hour of it is likely worth thousands of dollars. So asking for their time when no relationship exists is basically the same as asking for a $50,000 sale when no relationship exists. It's not going to happen—and even if it does, they won't bite on your high-end service just from that one call. Use an opt-in message instead and go from there.

WHAT TO SEND FOR YOUR COLD MESSAGE

There is an art to crafting lead generation messages. The more you hone your skill at creating scripts, the greater the conversion rates you will see on your messages. It's not only the specifics of the message that are important. The tone of your message can play a big part in how well your message converts.

It might be tempting to craft a very formal and professional message, but as with your LinkedIn messaging campaigns, it actually works better to loosen up your tone and try to write something more casual. Use a casual tone, like how you'd approach a close friend or family member. That's how you want the prospect to view you. You are trying to give the prospect the impression that you genuinely just came across their info and wanted to reach out, not that they are in a mass marketing campaign.

Let's look at an example regarding the tone of your message. Below are two intros to cold messages:

Dear Sir,

I am quite pleased to share with you a valuable resource that you may find of great use for your business. Please find it attached.

Vs.

Hey Bob,

I came across your profile in the Social Media Marketing group here on LinkedIn and thought you might be interested in a webinar coming up next week that I think is right up your alley. Here's the link. Hope you get some good stuff from it!

Which one sounds more appealing? It's a no-brainer.

A real person would never use the tone from the first example when sending a message to someone they know. In fact, the tone in the first example gives off a cold and impersonal vibe. The recipient would read that message and think, "I don't know this person, why should I listen to them? I'm tuning out."

Now, the prospect who receives the second message doesn't know the sender either, but the language is a lot more inviting and personal. The casual tone makes it easy for the recipient to take the message at face value and not think it was written and delivered by a robot from some company's marketing department. The second message was definitely written and sent by a *real person*. That will make all the difference.

SIZE MATTERS

Just as important as the tone is the length of the message. Do you think everyone will be interested to read nineteen paragraphs that outline your entire history and all of the services that you provide? Think again. Prospects will delete that message before they even finish the first sentence.

It's not just high-level executives at big companies whose time is valuable. *Everyone's* time is valuable. Do you read a super-long promotional email from someone you have never heard of before? No, you don't. You do the same thing everyone else does when they get that type of message: DELETE.

It doesn't make sense to send the type of cold message that you personally would scrap when you see it. Don't fall into the trap of thinking that just because a cold message is about *your* company that everyone else will think it's awesome. They'll think it's trash just like the rest.

Personal messages, messages from people who care, are not long. They are short, simple, to the point and casual. Let's check out an example of a message trying to get someone on a webinar:

SUBJECT: *Free LinkedIn Training for Financial Advisors*

Jane - We're both in the Finance Club group and I came across your profile this morning. I thought you might be interested in a free, LIVE, training event, specific for Financial Advisors, my company is hosting on March 10th. It's called How to Create a Massive Referral Network on LinkedIn with THE Most Influential Players in your Market.

This is not just theory. We will go through real examples of businesses just like yours that are taking a proactive approach to LinkedIn and, in turn, generating some awesome results.

If you're interested in more info on the webinar, topics scheduled for discussion, and to register, please visit this link:

>>INSERT LINK<<

Please feel free to forward this to anybody in your firm that would be interested. Hope to see you on the call.

Thanks,

Josh

There are a lot of great things happening in that script. The length is not super long, making it easily digestible for the recipient. It's straightforward and to the point. It lets the recipient know exactly what they are getting. There's no other fluff attached to the message. The subject line is straight to the point as well. No guessing game needed to figure out what this is about.

The language in the message is also tailored to fit the prospect. The recipient, a financial advisor, knows that this is specifically for them. This is not just some general webinar. This is going to be material specific and valuable to the recipient. They see the benefit.

Do not overcomplicate a cold message. It's easy and tempting to write a message much more complex than the one above. Don't do it. Keeping things simple and to the point is the key to your success.

HOW TO GET YOUR MESSAGE OUT TO THE MASSES

As mentioned previously, the cold message approach is typically a numbers game, which means that the key is *volume*. Cold messaging will not have the same conversion rate as a nurture campaign, but what it lacks in conversion rate it will make up for in scale. So you need to be able to hit thousands of people for this tactic to work.

If you have a prospect pool of only a couple hundred people, then this may not be the best approach. But if your prospect pool is tens of thousands or even hundreds of thousands, then you are on the right track for cold messaging to be effective. The larger the prospect pool, the more effective this approach can be.

Where can you go to deliver cold messages to thousands of targets?

I bet you already know: LinkedIn Groups.

LinkedIn makes getting access to the masses super easy. There are groups that cater to just about every single industry and niche you can think of, and many of the groups have thousands of members in them. Because you can send a message to anyone you share a group with, all it takes is joining a group that caters to your target, going into the group membership area, conducting a keyword search to narrow down who you want to send messages to specifically, and then start firing away.

This process is similar to fishing in the ocean with a giant net. You cast your net into the ocean, in an area where you know the fish hang out that *you* want to catch. Might you catch a few fish that are not the right types? Sure, but by and large, if you're in the right place, you'll find the right fish. Focus on the rule, not the exception. If you're getting a large volume of prospects to bite on your call to action, then you have your process zeroed in.

The number of people needed to bite on your call to action will be different for each business. One person may just need twenty people to show up to a webinar. Another person may need 300 people to opt-in for a report. Either way, cold messaging can work in both of those situations; you just need to determine how much activity it will take for you to hit your goal, and then do it.

In terms of sending out a significant volume of messages, it all comes down to having a process. Being able to copy and paste scripts quickly into messaging windows that you have opened up on your browser will save you a ton of time. Tedious? You bet. Effective? Hell yes!

You also don't need to do this activity yourself. An assistant or marketing team member can easily handle this type of activity once a group search has been identified and the script has been drafted.

Review the results, make adjustments, and keep firing away. Cold messaging might be the best play for you and your business. If it's a good fit for you, do not ignore it. It's too powerful of a play to let slip by.

CONCLUSION

Where to Start

You made it! Congrats on finishing this book. You now know how to leverage LinkedIn and webinars to supercharge your business, generate thousands of amazing leads, build relationships, establish yourself as an industry leader, and automate your systems to keep your growth going for years to come. Soon your business will be growing faster than ever!

I've thrown a ton of information at you in these pages. And it may seem like a lot to grasp. But don't panic! I promise you this will all start to make sense as soon as you begin taking steps to put the pieces in place. The best way to really learn these strategies and techniques is by jumping in with both feet. So I'm going to wrap this book up by sharing my favorite tips and tricks for getting started successfully.

TAKE IT SLOW

We've talked about a number of techniques and strategies in this book, and I recommend you try them all. But do *not* try to do them all at the same time right out of the gate. Ease into them. If you take on too many new projects all at once it will be harder to get them all on track. You'll probably get frustrated.

So start with one technique from this book, get it up and running, smooth it out, learn it well, and then go on to another. Take your time. You'll get to them all eventually.

YOU HAVE TO START SOMEWHERE

Knowing where to start is important. Which technique should you pick first? Think about what makes sense for you. Was there a strategy in this book that piqued your interest more than the others? What got you the most excited? Do you already have a lot of experience at LinkedIn? Have you ever hosted a webinar before? Do you like webinars? Are you good at making presentations? All of these types of questions can help you find the best starting point for you and your business.

Also think about where your company is likely to get the fastest results. Where do you think the most low-hanging fruit is for your business? How are you most likely going to reach your best prospects? Where will you get the greatest ROI? If you already spend two hours a day on LinkedIn, then launching a LinkedIn campaign may be the best starting point for you. If you already have a webinar that you've presented and recorded, maybe that's the best place to start.

If you're still not sure after you've thought through these questions, we recommend starting with the LinkedIn strategies first. This way you don't have the pressure of creating a sixty-minute webinar and marketing it in a month. Start with the LinkedIn messaging campaigns and creating your own LinkedIn group, where you can go at your own pace. Once you begin building your group, you'll gain confidence, and soon you'll be implementing the more advanced strategies, too.

HIRING AN AGENCY

One quick thought on hiring an agency or another company to outsource some of these campaigns and strategies. Be careful. There are hundreds of digital marketing consultants and new media ad agencies out there, but the vast majority of them are generalists—companies that do a little bit of everything but haven't really *mastered* the strategies discussed in this book. If you ask them whether they can implement a LinkedIn strategy or a webinar program for you, they'll always say yes to get your business...and then they'll have to go figure out how to do it on the fly. This is not what you want.

Don't trust a generalist social media agency or digital marketing firm to achieve the type of results described in this book. Instead, find a specialist who really knows this space. The strategies I've created and written about in this book are based on very focused, specific processes that took years to develop. They've proven to be effective through concrete results and ongoing optimization. And they're *all* we do. If you see the value in what these programs can do for your business, but you really don't have the internal resources or bandwidth to do it yourself, I'd love to talk about how we can work together. You can sign up for a complimentary strategy session at **LinkedSelling.com/Contact**, call our office at 314-499-8892, or email me at **JoshTurner@LinkedSelling.com**.

LET'S GET STARTED

It all comes back to this. Regardless of *where* you start, the most important thing is that you *make* a start. Set a date on your calendar to begin, and stick to it. Clear your calendar on that day so you can really dive in and focus on only this.

Just like starting anything else new, it comes down to making a commitment to moving forward, doing the work, learning as you go, and then cranking it up. I have no doubt that very soon you'll be using these strategies to turn thousands of cold prospects into warm leads and growing your business in a big way.

ACKNOWLEDGMENTS

There are many people that have played a big part in the journey that has led to the book you have in your hands today, including: Bill Croghan, Ben Kniffen, Jessica Wood, The Cohen Family, Jamie Kreft, Ryan Farrell, Margaret Muir, Alison Baker and the entire LinkedSelling team, David Gonzales, Bill Prenatt, Russ Henneberry, Oscar Turner, Brandon Dempsey, Jim Canada, Corey McDonald, Eddy Tauk, my Mom and Dad, my brother Joel, Rhonda Croghan, Ronald and Blanche Flynn, Aaron Agius, Tom Swip, Zach Obront, Chris Balish, and Lydia Turner.

And last but certainly not least, every single client of ours, every single member of Linked University, all of our partners, and the tens of thousands of people who have been through our trainings over the years.

This book doesn't exist without you, and I'm forever grateful.

ABOUT THE AUTHOR

Josh Turner is the founder of **Linked Selling,** a B2B marketing firm specializing in fully outsourced LinkedIn lead generation campaigns. They represent clients (like Neil Patel and Microsoft, to name a couple) in the US, Canada, UK, Asia, and Australia, in a wide variety of industries.

Josh's company also operates **LinkedUniversity.com,** an online training program for LinkedIn marketing. He is considered one of the leading experts in the world when it comes to growing your business using LinkedIn.

Made in the USA
Middletown, DE
14 November 2018